P9-DMI-891

WHERE MERCY FAILS

Darfur's Struggle to Survive

Text by Chris Herlinger
Photographs and Afterword by Paul Jeffrey

Seabury Books
NEW YORK

Copyright © 2009 by Chris Herlinger and Paul Jeffrey

Photos copyright © 2009 by Paul Jeffrey

All rights reserved. No part of this book may be reproduced, stored in a retrieval system, or transmitted in any form or by any means, electronic, mechanical, including photocopying, recording, or otherwise, without the written permission of the publisher.

Unless otherwise noted, the Scripture quotations contained herein are from the New Revised Standard Version Bible, copyright © 1989 by the Division of Christian Education of the National Council of Churches of Christ in the U.S.A. Used by permission. All rights reserved.

ISBN: 978-1-59627-102-9

Library of Congress Cataloging-in-Publication Data

Herlinger, Chris.
Where mercy fails : Darfur's struggle to survive/text, Chris Herlinger; photos and text, Paul Jeffrey.
p. cm.

ISBN 978-1-59627-102-9 (pbk.)
1. Famines—Sudan—Darfur. 2. Food relief—Sudan—Darfur. I. Jeffrey, Paul. II. Title
HC835.Z9F342 2009
363.809627—dc22

2008051350

Seabury Books
445 Fifth Avenue
New York, New York 10016
www.seaburybooks.com
An imprint of Church Publishing Incorporated
5 4 3 2 1

Printed in Canada

Deliver up the crown and to take mercy
On the poor souls for whom this hungry war
Opens his vasty jaws, and on your head
Turning the widows' tears, the orphans' cries,
The dead men's blood, the pining maidens' groans,
For husbands, fathers, and betrothed lovers,
That shall be swallowed in this controversy.

— William Shakespeare,
Act 2, Scene 4, *Henry V*

(Humanity) must learn the paradox that the world offers us a choice, not between good and evil, but between one evil and another....

— Dietrich Bonhoeffer, "What is a Christian Ethic?" (1929)

A reign of terror has often about it the atmosphere of farce. The irresponsible is in control.

— Graham Greene, "Nightmare Republic" from *Reflections* (1990)

Contents

Foreword

Where Mercy Fails is not an easy read. The authors record personal narratives of suffering, they take the reader into camps where displaced persons eke out a meager existence bereft of hope, and they tell of conflicts between humanitarian and human rights workers. They also give an explanation of some of the probable causes of this horrific tragedy. On a more hopeful note they review possible scenarios whereby the conflict might be resolved and the suffering alleviated. However, Herlinger and Jeffrey are under no illusions—this humanitarian crisis has intractable dimensions that make easy answers elusive.

Although the situation in Darfur-Chad has been widely publicised, public awareness has not galvanized the political will to bring sufficient pressure to bear on the government of Sudan to halt the violence. Global calls to put an end to what many describe as genocide have been empty. Women continue to be raped when they leave camp to collect firewood, and the abductions and murders on a horrific scale are carried out by warlords with impunity.

Where Mercy Fails brings us face to face with the human dimensions of this crisis and the socio-economic and political difficulties in trying to address it, as well as the implications for people of faith. I commend *Where Mercy Fails* as required reading for all caring people who wish to understand this intractable problem and who want to give an informed moral response.

Archbishop Desmond Tutu
Nobel Peace Prize Laureate

Acknowledgments

Our access to the narratives of despair and hope we relay here would not have been possible without the collaboration of many people working with humanitarian agencies. Yet Darfur remains a dangerous place to work, so we are not naming here those brave colleagues from all over the world who assisted us. They—especially the Africans—are the heroes of organized compassion in places like Sudan and Chad and elsewhere on the continent, and their commitment inspired us, their insight enlightened us, and their patience and good humor afforded us remarkable access to the survivors of the region's brutality.

We also thank our colleagues in the media where some of this material originally appeared (in often quite different forms), including *The Christian Century,* Catholic News Service, Ecumenical News International, *National Catholic Reporter,* Religion News Service, and *Response.* We would also like to thank our editor at Seabury Books, Davis Perkins, who conceived this project and calmly shepherded it through serially delayed deadlines.

From Chris: I'm deeply thankful to my friends and current and former colleagues at Church World Service for their unflagging support, including Rick Augsburger, Donna J. Derr, John McCullough, Joanne Rendall, Ann Walle, and my fellow CWS emergency response and communications staffers. A word of thanks as well to those who read this manuscript at various stages—CWS staff members; a group of Yale Divinity School students; dear friend and running partner Ruth Gursky, who read with a smart set of objective eyes; and equally dear friend Elizabeth Haak, a wonderfully thorough and exacting copyeditor who patiently saw this project through several drafts. Her dedication was a marvel.

Also thanks to journalist friends and colleagues who have provided help and guidance through the years, sometimes at critical times, including David E. Anderson, Nils Carstensen, Richard Nelson, the late Ronald Ross, Gus Spohn, Tom Weber, and Frank Wright. Thanks also to Juan Carlos Davila, *periodista y amigo fiel.*

Time to reflect and write is precious, and my thanks also go to the Harvard Divinity School, where I spent a sabbatical in the spring of 2005 as a resident fellow and worked on the first articles that became the genesis for this text; and to Yale Divinity School, where I was a visiting fellow in 2008. YDS offered a congenial and quiet environment in which to write. I was, and am, far from a perfect student, but I hope my friends and teachers from Denver East High School, Macalester College, Union Theological Seminary, and Cambridge University will find some of my commitment to learning in these pages. A special thanks to formative teachers David Hopper, Sara Katz, Emily and

Norman Rosenberg, and Robert Warde. Also to Vincent Wimbush and other members of the Union faculty, and to Charles Jones of Cambridge.

I dedicate this book to my parents, David and Lynn Herlinger, and to my sister, Rebecca Herlinger, for their unqualified love, support and boundless humor, all of which keep me grounded, and to the memory of my late brother, Matthew Herlinger. Matt was not a traveler, but as an artist he would have appreciated this book's fusion of writing and photography.

From Paul: I can travel and write because I have colleagues and editors who make that possible, and who encourage me to go deeper into each story. They include Mike Dubose, Steve Goldstein, John Goodwin, Dana Jones, Callie Long, Yvette Moore, Barbara Wheeler, and many others. Thanks to all of you. Keep pushing me.

Thanks also to Lucas and Abi for pulling me home from wherever I roam with their own adventures that make me proud. Thanks to Lyda, whose love still makes me giddy. And profound thanks to my parents—Fran and David—for teaching me to be curious about this wonderful world.

Introduction

Then the Lord said to Cain, "Where is your brother Abel?"
He said, "I do not know; am I my brother's keeper?"
And the Lord said, "What have you done?
Listen; your brother's blood is crying out to me from the ground!"

— Gen. 4:9–10

The valley that stretches north from the Bela Mountains turns deep green every year when the rains come to Darfur. Any farmer would love the wide, well-watered valley, and indeed you can see faint outlines of fields where donkey-drawn plows once turned the soil over seeds of sorghum and peanuts. But there are no farmers or donkeys these days, just an occasional herd of camels, a herder or two lingering in the shadows of the trees along the wadi that absorbs the afternoon thunderstorms. There are also no farmers' homes, only the decaying circles of mud that were once the walls of huts whose thatched roofs sheltered the laughing children of the Fur tribe.

The village, called Bela like the mountains, has been quiet since a December 2003 attack by Arab militias that killed thirty-seven people and drove the terrorized survivors into camps for the internally displaced outside the nearby cities of Garsila and Deleij. Its silence is the sound of genocide in slow motion, and the grass and weeds growing up amidst the skeletons of burned huts are proof that the world has not cared enough to stop the violence and bring the people of Bela home.

The people of Bela were farmers. In the culturally bifurcated landscape of Darfur, they consider themselves Africans, different from the Arab nomads who drove them away. To the outsider they seem similar—both are dark-skinned, both Muslim, and both speak Arabic. But their cultural differences—like those of Cain and Abel, farmer and herder—fill centuries of Darfur history with alternating periods of tension and peaceful coexistence. And it was those cultural differences that were exploited by the central government in Khartoum when it felt threatened by a nascent rebel movement that began to demand something better for the long marginalized communities in the Texas-sized westernmost region of Sudan. The government pushed the nomads to fight the farmers, providing arms and money and intelligence and Antonov bombers to accompany the raids. As a result, at least two hundred and fifty thousand and perhaps as many as four hundred thousand people are dead, and some 2.5 million displaced within Darfur or living as refugees across the border in Chad. More than 4 million Darfurians are directly affected by the violence, and hundreds of villages like Bela lie abandoned, their charred ruins slowly being reclaimed by the desert.

This book is an exercise in journalism, both in words and images, about the nature of the Darfur crisis and the failure of governments and international institutions, despite considerable pressure from activists, many from faith communities, to set it right. It is a complicated story, and we don't pretend to present a definitive history or a comprehensive visual record. This is simply a glimpse of what we have seen and heard on assignments to Darfur and Chad between 2004 and 2008, and a reflection on what that means for the international community.

We both work with church-based humanitarian agencies, and admit to having a bias that many journalists and certainly all humanitarian workers possess: a bias in favor of the victims of political violence and abuse. We acknowledge this prejudice, yet we are not blind to the complexities of Sudan and the cruel realities of international politics, nor to the tricky claims of grievance held by those seeking political change, nor even to the occasionally contradictory witness of the survivors themselves.

We realize that the situation in Darfur has deep roots in colonial legacies and looming environmental crises, and we know that the interplay of political forces in the region has only grown increasingly complicated in the years since the first shots were fired in 2003. Yet what remains strikingly clear for us is that Darfur is not merely a humanitarian crisis. Although it remains the largest humanitarian operation in the world, the massive exercise of organized mercy has failed to resolve the crisis, which is deeply economic, political, cultural, and environmental in nature. Clearly, compassion can but temper the suffering of some. Moreover, the limits imposed on humanitarian action by the government in Khartoum further hamper the world's response. Aid agencies and workers in the field are passionate about the need for something more than organized compassion, yet they often understandably reserve public comment so as not to jeopardize their access to the displaced.

What they say privately is that only concerted international pressure will stop the manufacture of more victims. Such a response, however, has not materialized. Until recently, Europe slept through the ethnic cleansing and Arab countries looked the other way. The role of the United States was conflicted; the U.S. government was uncomfortable with the violence but did not want to risk losing the intelligence on Al-Qaeda it was getting from people like Salah Abdalla Gosh, a former lieutenant to Osama bin Laden who is today the head of Sudan's secret police and one of the main architects of the government's scorched earth counterinsurgency program. And given its occupation of Iraq, the United States had little political capital to expend intervening in a conflict in another largely Muslim country.

China has been the most significant outside player in the Darfur tragedy. A permanent member of the United Nations Security Council, it made sure that a UN-sponsored African Union peacekeeping mission, on the ground in Darfur since 2004, suffered from such a weak mandate that by most accounts it ended up only making matters worse, becoming a target itself for attacks. These days China seems to be backing the wrong guys throughout Africa, simply because they have resources; from Sudan it gets more than 7 percent of the oil it needs for its growing economy. Encouraged by activist film stars who began threatening a boycott of the Beijing Olympics, the Chinese government began in 2007 to modify its rigid support for Khartoum's policies, a change that led to the deployment that year of a new UN peacekeeping force to take over from the beleaguered AU mission.

Yet the presence of those twenty-six thousand soldiers and police, if the UN force is ever fully deployed, will be limited by their lack of authority to seize weapons from the constantly multiplying roster of belligerents, as well as by the absence of any provision for sanctioning the Khartoum regime if it continues its noncompliance with Security Council resolutions. Neither is the UN force mandated to deal with the spillover of violence into neighboring Chad and the Central African Republic. The increasingly regional character of the Darfur conflict—genocide without borders, according to some—has highlighted the inability of the UN to intervene in a timely and effective manner.

A key question begs to be asked in the belabored debates about the UN force and its slow deployment: exactly what peace are these peacekeepers supposed to be keeping? In places like Bela, it is definitely peaceful today, but only because the residents of Bela are crowded into camps for the internally displaced. Even though most of the African farming villages in Darfur have already been destroyed, government bombings, Arab militia raids, and rebel attacks continued through 2008. The government and its proxies are apparently determined to dislodge those who still dare cling to their huts and farms, while the rebels are determined to keep the violence going until something changes the unequal equation of power inside Sudan. (The rebels' own acts of violence have earned them criticism from human rights groups and, in November 2008, prompted the International Criminal Court to seek rebel arrests for the murders of a dozen AU peace-keepers.)

Meanwhile, crowded camps for the displaced have reached such size that relief officials now seek sites for new camps. The ineffectiveness of the peacekeepers is so obvious that some have asked if the deployment of the AU troops and then their conversion into a UN force was merely a costly exercise in helping the international community feel like it was doing something. While the world's guilt may have been assuaged, the mass murder in Darfur never stopped.

The violence in Darfur does not happen in a vacuum. External factors—from China's energy colonialism and Muammar Gaddafi's Arab identity politics to encroaching desertification—all loom in the background. And factors within Sudan—from the long and extremely violent conflict in the south, the resolution of which served as partial inspiration for Darfur's guerrillas at the beginning of this decade, to the centralized control exercised by the economic and political elites along the Nile—also play their part. Deciphering the individual elements of this complex weave of narratives is not simple. Darfur is not an easy place to get to and there is nothing approaching a scholarly consensus on the region's ills, much less its future.

Given the sweep of the violence in Darfur, most forecasts are not optimistic. Yet Alex de Waal, a fellow at Harvard's Global Equity Initiative, argues that the Sudanese "have an extraordinary capacity to reconcile" that should not be discounted. Some faith-based relief efforts in Darfur are seeking to capitalize on that capacity by nurturing grassroots conflict resolution skills. Moreover, some analysts suggest that the breakdown since 2007 of the dominant primary narrative of government-induced ethnic conflict—a few Arab militias, for example, feeling used by Khartoum, have turned against the government, even forming common alliances with African rebel groups—bodes well for pressuring recalcitrant parties toward negotiations. Yet many others see only deepening chaos with no discernable end—a literal anarchy that only serves to strengthen Khartoum's dominance. Meanwhile, as the conflict simmers on and hope withers for an eventual return home from the burgeoning camps for the displaced and refugees, bitterness flourishes amid the tents and straw shelters, nourishing resentment and anger that may fuel armed conflict long into the future.

Does the violence in Darfur constitute genocide? Some claim it fails to meet the strict definition of the 1948 Convention on the Prevention and Punishment of the Crime of Genocide, summed up in the Convention as an "intent to destroy, in whole or in part, a national, ethnical, racial or religious group, as such." A 2005 UN report argued that in the case of Darfur, "genocidal intent appears to be missing." Yet the same report warned that this conclusion "should not be taken in any way as detracting from the gravity of… the crimes against humanity and war crimes that have been committed in Darfur [and which] may be no less serious and heinous than genocide."

The government of Sudan has systematically denied the accusations of genocide, especially after the 2008 action by the International Criminal Court to indict Sudanese President Omar Hassan al-Bashir for genocide, war crimes, and crimes against humanity in Darfur.

Whether we can call it genocide is not a mere exercise in semantics. The international community, under the rubric of its doctrine on the "responsibility to protect"—often referred to in humanitarian circles by the shorthand "R2P"—is *required* to intervene to protect civilians whose security cannot be guaranteed by their own government. Yet in the years since the R2P was adopted by the UN in 2005, the violence in Darfur has been a damning indictment of the international community's predilection for empty words.

More important than whether the violence constitutes genocide or not is the nagging question of whether we have done enough to stop it. Never has so much attention been paid to a campaign of violence like this while it was still in process. Never has there been so much public clamor for the world to put an end to a genocide in progress. And yet all the protests, all the "Not on Our Watch" bracelets, all the prayer vigils and letters to politicians, at the end of the day, have done little to change the situation on the ground. The question that remains is not whether what is happening in Darfur is genocide. It is why we allow the violence, whatever we call it, to continue.

Paul Jeffrey
Eugene, Oregon

Chris Herlinger
New York City

December 2008

1

A Cry from Darfur

The blame is only against those who oppress men and wrong-doing and insolently transgress beyond bounds through the land, defying right and justice: for such there will be a penalty grievous.

— The Holy Qur'an 42:42

During the dry, hot, sunny days of December, they looked longingly at the hills where they once farmed, raised families, and buried their kin. While recounting their experiences in camps they had grown to hate, they were surrounded by the very men who had driven them to the perdition the rest of the world now simply knows as Darfur. In villages not far from Garsila in West Darfur, the killings and shootings in October 2003 were drawn out over four agonizing hours. In one hamlet, sixty-eight people were murdered. A month later, in another nearby area, flame throwers and matches were the weapons of choice: some two hundred villagers were forced into blazing huts and burned alive. In the city of Um Kher, a conscience-stricken man lucky enough to have escaped brutalities himself, recalled his efforts to stop the bloodletting. Warned about a January 2004 attack on the village of Kanyou, he called local authorities to alert them to the violence that eventually left some one hundred dead. But he was crisply told it was outside their area of control and that the authorities would not respond. "We could hear it here," said the man, nearly a full year later, standing in the shadows of a deserted village square. "The Janjaweed surrounded the village and they shot anybody who tried to escape." He later realized the futility of his act. "They were sent to kill people, not to save people."

The stories—and there are many more like these—follow a nearly identical pattern: para-militaries known as the Janjaweed arrived on camels and horses, working in tandem with Sudanese government troops in trucks and cars. They looted the hamlets, murdered the men, and raped the women. The attacks were often preceded by aerial bombardments by Russian-made Antonov aircraft.

For the survivors who recounted the atrocities, the stories are, in a sense, unfinished: those in the fetid camps find themselves being watched, policed, and bullied by the same authorities and surrounded by the same paramilitaries. The result is benumbing shock, fear, and trauma, a collective weariness of spirit and body. "The only thing they [the authorities] have done is grudgingly granted us permission to feed people," said one exasperated European aid worker. "But they still feel they have the right to harass and kill." More than 2 million people in Darfur and neighboring Chad are experiencing such debasement, spending their days in what amounts to concentration camps. Many burn with baleful, hateful memories and have no immediate hope of ever returning to life as it was. "The people in the camps," said a Norwegian humanitarian worker, "are stuck between a past they don't want to remember and a future they cannot see or even glimpse."

A Darfur Primer

What Are the Causes?

The immediate cause was the attack, in 2003, on government targets by a rebel group known as the Sudan Liberation Army (SLA), and the resulting response by the Sudanese government. A second group, the Justice and Equality Movement (JEM), was allied with the SLA for a time, but the two groups have since split, in part because both groups have distinct ethnic identities. JEM has also embraced a distinct Islamic identity. Despite differences, however, both groups argue that the Khartoum government has systematically ignored Darfur, which means "land of the Fur" and is not a single province, but a region containing three states: North, South, and West Darfur. The rebel groups also allege that the government has favored the rights of nomadic Arab tribes over the rights of the Fur, Masalit, and Zaghawa tribes in such matters as land disputes.

What Toll Has the Conflict Taken?

More than 2.5 million people have fled from their homes and been forced into displacement or refugee camps by the attacks by Sudanese government troops and their allies, the *Janjaweed* militias. However, even approximate numbers of those who have died—either killed outright or perished from resulting food shortages and disease—remain in dispute. At the very least, two hundred and fifty thousand, and perhaps as many as four hundred thousand are believed to have perished. The four hundred thousand figure is contested, though in late 2008, the figure of three hundred thousand was being used by some UN officials.

Who Are the *Janjaweed*?

They are perhaps the most notorious symbol of the violence in Darfur. An older definition of *Janjaweed* was used for bandits who would "form, raid, and flee." Many believe that the new *Janjaweed* are, in fact, not only allied with the Sudanese government, but a creation of the Sudanese government. Musa Hilal, a key *Janjaweed* leader, has publicly declared that he and others have taken their orders from the Sudanese government. A Sudanese military official said in 2004 the *Janjaweed* were "recruited, equipped, and paid" by the Khartoum government because so many in the Sudanese armed forces are from Darfur and would not uproot or terrorize their own people.

What Is the Role of Ethnic Identity?

The role of ethnicity remains controversial. To those attacked by the *Janjaweed* militias, embracing an "African" identity is crucial. They believe they have been victimized because they are non-Arab. However, some experts, like author and researcher Alex de Waal argue that the "Arab-African dichotomy" is the result of political ideology—in part due to a growing ideology of Arab "supremacy" that spread across the region and was fostered by Libyan leader Muammar Gaddafi in the 1980s.

Another scholar, Francis Deng, has noted that "identity cuts across all the issues and is therefore the central strand in the web" of Sudan's recent history. He argues that Sudan's crisis of national identity "emanates from the fact that the politically dominant.... northern Sudanese Arabs, although the products of Arab-African genetic mixing and a minority in the country as a whole, see themselves as primarily Arab, deny the African element in them, and seek to impose their self-perceived identity throughout the country...." This ruling Arab minority, Deng argues, "seeks to define the national character along the lines of their self-perception, itself a distortion of their composite identity as a mixed Arab-African race in which the African element is more visible but actively denied."

Are There Differences between "Arab" and "*Janjaweed*"?

Yes. A January 2005 report of a UN inquiry on Darfur said: "The fact that the *Janjaweed* are described as Arab militias does not imply that all Arabs are fighting on the side of the *Janjaweed*." In fact, the UN report said many Arabs in Darfur are opposed to the *Janjaweed*, while some Arabs are even fighting with the Darfur rebels opposed to the Khartoum government. The report said: "At the same time, many non-Arabs are supporting the government and serving its army. Thus, the term *Janjaweed* referred to by victims in Darfur certainly does not mean 'Arabs' in general, but rather Arab militias raiding their villages and committing other violations."

What Is Muammar Gaddafi's Role in the Area?

Writing in the London-based *Guardian* newspaper in 2007, journalist Julian Borger said that the region's leaders "have sought to turn hardship to their advantage." That includes Gaddafi, who has tried to become a regional peacemaker. That is ironic, Borger notes, because during the 1980s Gaddafi formed an "Islamic Legion" from various ethnic groups, including nomads, and "used them to try to carve out an 'Arab belt' across Chad and into (Darfur and Sudan) under his sway." Though Gaddafi's forces, Borger writes, "were soundly beaten by the Chadian army in 1987 . . . numbers of the legionnaires hung around the area—armed, trained, and imbued with ideas of Arab (supremacy), looking for the next fight. Many are now leading *Janjaweed* raiders into battle."

What Is the Role of the Environment?

UN Secretary General Ban Ki-moon declared in 2007 that climate change was a possible cause of the Darfur conflict because the reduction in rainfall in western Sudan had caused nomadic groups to look for land elsewhere in Darfur. Some people have even gone so far as to say that Darfur is the world's first "climate change" war. "Those who were prepared to kill, rape, and pillage were drawn from the ranks of the desperate, ripped from their traditional way of life by a catastrophic change in the weather," Julian Borger wrote in 2007. "Global warming created the dry tinder. Khartoum supplied the match." A related issue is that of land disputes. Alex de Waal has written that "land rights are key to understanding Darfur and the conflicts therein," adding, "The rapid using-up of free cultivable land and the degradation of the range meant that land disputes became more common and more bloody in the 1980s," laying a foundation for the present conflict.

How Does Genocide Figure into the Conflict?

In July 2008, Luis Moreno-Ocampo, the chief prosecutor at the International Criminal Court in the Hague, asked that Sudanese President Omar Hassan al-Bashir be arrested for ten counts of "genocide, crimes against humanity, and war crimes." The arrest warrant was requested because, Moreno-Ocampo charged, al-Bashir allegedly "masterminded and implemented a plan to destroy in substantial part the Fur, Masalit, and Zaghawa groups, on account of their ethnicity. His motives were largely political. His alibi was a 'counterinsurgency.' His intent was genocide."

The international legal definition of genocide is found in Articles II and III of the 1948 Convention on the Prevention and Punishment of Genocide. The articles are as follows:

> Article II: In the present Convention, genocide means any of the following acts committed with intent to destroy, in whole or in part, a national, ethnical, racial or religious group, as such:
>
> (a) Killing members of the group;
> (b) Causing serious bodily or mental harm to members of the group;
> (c) Deliberately inflicting on the group conditions of life calculated to bring about its physical destruction in whole or in part;
> (d) Imposing measures intended to prevent births within the group;
> (e) Forcibly transferring children of the group to another group.

Article III: The following acts shall be punishable:

(a) Genocide;

(b) Conspiracy to commit genocide;

(c) Direct and public incitement to commit genocide;

(d) Attempt to commit genocide;

(e) Complicity in genocide.

United States officials have used the term genocide to describe events in Darfur, a term that Europeans have been reluctant to embrace. This, some have theorized, is because it is difficult for European countries to take a unified position on Darfur given their commitment to a European Union policy that pledges EU members to "speak with one voice" on foreign policy matters. Writing in *The Washington Post* as the Darfur crisis unfolded in 2004, Christian W. D. Bock, a former legal adviser to the United Nations Economic Commission for Europe, and Leland R. Miller, a New York lawyer and member of the International Institute of Strategic Studies, said requiring such an "über-majority," in effect, "eliminates the possibility of collective armed intervention. By defect or design, this allows member states to voice their concerns—and then excuse their inaction as bowing to the judgment of the whole. In effect the European Union has fashioned a foreign policy mechanism by which inaction is virtually automatic—even in the face of genocide."

What Is the Sudanese Government's Position?

The Sudanese government has systematically denied the charges of genocide. President al-Bashir termed the request for his arrest "part of a neo-colonialist agenda to protect the interests of developed countries." (Sudan was once under British colonial rule.) Al-Bashir's government has used the same argument in opposing the deployment of UN troops in Darfur. The al-Bashir government has also denied a link with the *Janjaweed*. The government says the militias are no more than bandits who have long terrorized the Darfur countryside looking for bounty and that it has had no control over *Janjaweed* fighters. The government has also said it was within its right to battle an incipient insurgency that threatened the security of Darfur and the stability of Sudan.

What Are Other Theories about the Conflict?

In a 2004 interview, a Sudanese military official theorized, as have others, that forces within the government may not, at first, have had genocidal intent in Darfur but wanted to prevent the country from splintering. They "reacted out of fear" to events in Darfur, he said, at a time when the Khartoum government was engaged in sensitive negotiations over the conflict between northern and southern Sudan.

What Is the Nature of the North-South War?

A two-decades-long civil war—which pitted the northern Khartoum government against southern Sudan, a predominately animist and Christian region—resulted in the deaths of some 2 million people. Arguments about marginalization are common among both Darfuris and southerners, and the North-South war and resulting peace process served as a motivator for those in Darfur fighting the Khartoum government. A North-South peace agreement was signed in January 2005, and under the agreement, the northern government and former rebels from the Sudan People's Liberation Army (SPLA), a group not connected to Darfur, share power. A degree of autonomy was also granted to the south. The role of the special envoy, former Senator John Danforth, was praised as a model for a successful U.S. role in Sudan.

What Is the Nature of U.S.-Sudanese Relations?

The Darfur crisis occurred just at a time when the Sudanese government was beginning to develop a better relationship with the United States. Earlier, President Ronald Reagan made Sudan a strategic ally to counter the regional influence of Gaddafi. While the U.S.-Sudan relationship later deteriorated, it improved after the events of September 11, 2001, when the United States sought new allies. The U.S. stepped up its role in trying to resolve the North-South conflict, which had long been a concern to one of President George W. Bush's constituent bases—conservative evangelical Christians. Subsequent events in Darfur have caused serious tensions between the United States and Sudan, and there were disagreements within the Bush administration about how best to deal with Sudan. A particular concern was how closely the U.S. government should be allied with Sudan on matters of intelligence gathering.

What Is the Role of China in Sudan?

As part of its drive for markets for its goods and obtaining natural resources for its economic expansion, China has embarked on a policy of new alliances with African countries. One of them is Sudan. China exports military hardware to Sudan, and is the major buyer of Sudan's oil. China has been accused of contravening a UN arms embargo meant to prevent fueling further conflict in Darfur. One of the allegations, reported by the BBC in July 2008, is that China is actually training fighter pilots who use its A5 Fantan fighter jets in Darfur. China claims it has not violated any UN arms embargoes.

❖   ❖   ❖

"Genocide by Force of Habit"

There are other themes and dimensions that will be tackled within these pages, but one bears special attention: the nature of political power in Sudan. Alex de Waal has suggested that what has happened in Darfur is "the routine cruelty of a security cabal, its humanity withered by years of power.... It is a genocide by force of habit." How is that possible? Gérard Prunier, another Darfur analyst, has noted that Sudan has been no stranger to "permanent war." The Sudanese government's foundational philosophy and policy since coming to power in 1989, he argues, has "kept verging on genocide in its general treatment of the national question in Sudan....The practice of genocide or quasi-genocide in Sudan has never been a deliberate well-thought out policy but rather a spontaneous tool used for keeping together a 'country' which is under minority Arab domination and which is in fact one of the last multi-national empires on the planet."

The issue of spontaneity and improvising is key, writes Prunier, because the government of Sudan's governing style has always been marked by confusion—something "partly unintended and partly deliberate. Contradictions are useful since they allow subsequent denial by contrasting one pronouncement with another." This is one reason why the United States and other countries have had such difficulty dealing with the Khartoum government. For Americans and Europeans, "extreme evil is associated with tragedy and tragedy is serious," Prunier argues. "Genocide or ethnic cleansing is a deadly serious business, and the fact that it could be carried out in haphazard conditions was unthinkable for the decorous international community. The grotesque is not part of its conceptual equipment, and only late in the day did foreigners begin to realize that the horror was far from coherent."

Given this, there was no need, Prunier believes, for Sudan's leaders to deliberately plan Darfur's annihilation, as the Nazis had in destroying European Jewry. "The decision-makers understood each other without having to plan and plot," he writes. As a ruling group, they felt they faced a danger and responded accordingly—they "could not afford to be too choosy about the means.... The tools were readily available; they merely had to be upgraded. It was done, and the rest is now history."

2

A Tinderbox of War and Dread

This place dislocates everything.

— Toni Morrison, *Tar Baby* (1981)

When I first traveled to Darfur in late 2004, I was discouraged but not entirely surprised by what I saw. Anyone engaged in humanitarian work is no stranger to seeing the underside of life, and the sense of outward shock of those in Darfur's displacement camps reminded me of people I had met in other areas of conflict. It was obvious that this was an unusually brutal affair that had closed in on civilians in a particularly ugly way—people were living as if in a traumatized trance. There was also the element of scale to consider. Leaving Darfur in late 2004, on a helicopter used to ferry humanitarian personnel, it was hard not to be startled by the sheer immensity of what had happened. Only from the window of a helicopter or a plane was it possible to grasp the magnitude of displacement and loss: from such a vantage point, I could fully see how communities hosting tens of thousands of people driven from their homes had been inexorably altered.

The towns' boundaries are now expanded by rows of hundreds of tarps—both blue- and dust-colored—and clusters of encampments. From the air, the scope of devastation inflicted on small villages—either from outright destruction or abandonment—was best evinced: I could see the extent of the damage—scorched homes, evidence of bombings—to many of the villages destroyed or damaged in the unwanted spasms of violence that caused more than 2 million people to flee their communities.

Scale, of course, tells only part of the story. Consequences of events also have to be judged when seen up close. When some colleagues and I walked along the silent pathways of one of those abandoned villages it was eerily quiet. We were surrounded by damaged, vacant homes, and the natural surroundings were strangely stilled—we could not even hear bird or animal sounds. Given such conditions, it was easy to describe Darfur as a tinderbox of war and dread. Yet the description almost seemed to belie the hardscrabble nature of the place, not unlike the desert of the southwestern United States. Darfur is a barren land with little luminosity and few round edges, bereft of greenery except in a short rainy season and in some areas, like the mountains of Jebel Mara, where waterfalls and lush growth are found year-round. Darfur is notable most of all for its extremes of sun, heat, and, at times, ferocious winds. This is admittedly an outsider's description. It isn't necessarily the vision or memory of those uprooted who have left Darfur (many for neighboring Chad) or remain confined within Darfur's cramped displacement camps and are unable to return to their home villages.

For those like Rahkia Ismael Khatir, who lives in a refugee camp in eastern Chad, which borders Sudan, Darfur was a place where life was marked by difficulty and hardship, but it was also home. While Darfur was, and remains, a poor place, to those who lived there it was not a place of deprivation. Farming families like Khatir's could eke out a living in relative peace and with a degree of certainty. In Khatir's village of Kiyagnou in North Darfur, cattle were abundant, as were the vegetables and fruits Khatir remembers growing in family plots. Like other Darfur refugees, Khatir recalls her village's gardens with great specificity—hers produced corn, millet, watermelon, tomatoes, pepper, onion, okra, garlic, pumpkin, parsley, and lettuce. Her notably detailed list stands in marked contrast to the standard refugee diet of sorghum, flour, and cooking oil, augmented by vegetables grown in the smallest of plots. She and other refugees exchange these vegetables, as well as other food and clothing, in acts of kindness she describes as "African solidarity"—a sense of unity and cooperation among camp residents and particularly camp women, the hardest workers among the displaced.

Food and confinement are two marks of Khatir's changed world, and they carry with them the pangs of frustration and hurt. "I don't like this life, being dependent. I want to be free," she said. She doesn't like being restricted in her movements. In the quest for firewood for cooking, she and other women are threatened by those she calls "the children of Arabs." But the deeper hurt and frustration, bordering on anger and bitterness, is about the violence—the *political* violence, destruction, and death—she and her family witnessed, forcing them to flee their village. While no experience in Darfur can be called representative, Khatir's story is not uncommon. She and her husband, Hissen Thom Ismael, and four children, ages two to fourteen, fled their village in 2004 when the *Janjaweed*—some in civilian attire, others in military uniform—attacked Kiyagnou. While she does not recall casualty numbers, she does remember the disproportionate weaponry used in a village where guns were not part of everyday life:

"The war that took place was not with bow and arrow but with heavy weapons."

Khatir is still at a loss to explain *why* this happened, but believes it stems from government favoritism toward "the Arabs." She believes acts that began as small things—local authorities not prosecuting animal theft, land acquisitions—later culminated in the violence that did Khatir and her family and neighbors gross and malignant harm. "It's the government, the government that does not like us," she said emphatically and emotionally to me at eight in the morning, a time in May when the sunlight in equatorial Africa is as blazing as it is at noon. She paused a moment. "Maybe it's because we're poor, maybe because we're black." Another pause. "We don't have the voice with the government," she said, her anger rising. "The government turns a blind eye to us." Khatir continued, "We've been chased off our land." Under what conditions could she envision returning to her village? "Get rid of the government," she said, her hands chopping the air. I asked her if there was any chance she and others could be reconciled with the Arabs. "We will never, *ever* reconcile with the Arabs," she said. "They destroyed our villages, killed our fathers and husbands, and raped our sisters." She paused. "Reconciliation? Never, ever."

Power as Persuasion; Attendant Tragedy

The violent intrusion of naked political power into the daily life of those like Khatir is one way to explain the Darfur conflict. But another definition of power—power as *persuasion*, as moral influence—is also part of the Darfur narrative. Concerned citizens throughout the world are outraged by what happened in Darfur. Many have embraced activism to try to stop it; many are young and many are acting either out of commitment to secular humanitarian values or the ethical values of the world's great religious traditions. For these activists, Darfur has come to symbolize the chance to right the wrongs the world ignored in Rwanda a decade earlier. It is, they argue, the chance for the international community—which has gone on record saying it has a responsibility to protect civilians against massive violations of human rights—to set things right.

Unfortunately, the world has not set things right, at least not in time to prevent or stem further atrocities in Darfur. The international community has not yet foresworn the long-stated primacy of sovereignty for the newer agenda of "responsibility to protect." The world has reacted, as it usually does in these circumstances, treating Darfur not as a political problem but as a humanitarian problem, with decidedly mixed results: success (many lives saved, by all accounts) and attendant tragedy (political inaction that likely caused many deaths). "It's apples and oranges; they're separate things," said John Prendergast, a prominent antigenocide activist. "Humanitarian aid deals with the succor of civilians, easing people's suffering, and that is needed. But to fully end what is happening in Darfur, we have to focus on diplomacy and prosecute those who have committed genocide." Fellow activist Chad Hazlett, of the Genocide Intervention Network, put it this way: "Humanitarian assistance has been an enormous success in saving lives, but it doesn't address the core problems. When you're feeding the people who fled the storm, you're not stopping the storm." Perhaps a better word is "whirlwind"—a whirlwind that began in 2003, and as of late 2008, shows no signs of letting up.

What Is *Darfur?*

How did all of this come to pass? How did a little-known and once largely ignored region in western Sudan the size of France suddenly become synonymous with what many call the first genocide of the twenty-first century?

The answers do not come readily. Events in Darfur continue to unfold; it is still not an easy place for journalists, aid workers, and other outsiders to enter; there is not anything approaching a scholarly consensus on the region or its history. At play: elements of politics (a feud by different parties over control of Darfur), environment (nomadic peoples from Sudan, Chad, and Libya being forced further south to eke out a living due to changes in the desert), grievance (long-standing neglect of Darfur by the central government), and identity (tangled and clashing visions of religion, ethnicity, and nationalism).

All of this is happening in a nation that itself remains highly contested: the crisis in Darfur has occurred against a backdrop of two decades of war in Sudan that has pitted an authoritarian government in Khartoum—often advocating a strict interpretation of Islam in the name of a national identity—against southern Sudan, a region in which many people practice Christianity and indigenous religions.

New York Times reporters Jeffrey Gettleman and Lydia Polgreen noted in a July 2008 dispatch from the capital of Khartoum: "Although the West has been relentlessly focused on Darfur, here in Sudan, most people view the crisis as simply a continuation of a long chain of internal conflicts between an autocratic government and the deeply impoverished people on the periphery. The deadliest of these conflicts, between the north and south, raged for decades, killing 2.2 million people—many more than the lives lost in Darfur—and threatened to split the country along religious lines."

The conjunction of nationalism and religion has been enormously destructive to the social fabric of Sudan. Writing about his country long before the crisis in Darfur, Francis Deng noted that the state's religious agenda has denied "democratic freedoms to Muslims and non-Muslims alike and has adopted strategies that have led to gross violations of international human rights standards, all of which negate the spiritual and ethical ideals normally associated with all religions."

Religion itself may not be an overt cause of the Darfur conflict—unlike the North-South conflict, those fighting each other in Darfur are all Muslim—but issues of identity, fueled by a legacy of government-imposed religious strictures, are now front and center in the conflict. Always a place of multiple and often-shifting identities in which labels such as "African" and "Arab" have been blurred because of intermarriage and easy comingling with neighbors, who you are and how others see you are now dynamics polarizing Darfur. The Darfur guerillas fighting the Sudanese government call themselves "African," while those victimized by the violence are likely to call any nomad who might be Arab a "*Janjaweed*."

An Encounter with the Guerrillas

Whatever its causes, the immediate spark that set off a war and a counterinsurgency campaign in Darfur began with young guerilla fighters. Some are barely out of their teens, some are younger. Most are under thirty. Yet with all the attention being heaped on Darfur during the early stages of the crisis, the motives of the rebel groups that precipitated the war—most notably the Sudan Liberation Army—remained murky. A *New York Times Magazine* piece by journalist Scott Anderson ascribed vague motives to the SLA—in Anderson's words, "a hazy list of grievances against Khartoum, most centering on the political and economic neglect of Darfur in general and the African tribes in particular."

Was Anderson right? Two colleagues and I weren't sure when we had an encounter with the SLA. We were only an hour's drive from the city of Nyala. Having been allowed safe passage in the region to get an idea of the humanitarian needs, we stayed in the village of Um Seifa, the site of a small medical clinic and a water station. We spoke to men and women who had been displaced and were using the village as a safe haven. We also spoke to the SLA members who patrolled the roads. They spoke passionately about the friends and relatives they had lost in the conflict, their frustrations with the Khartoum government, and the need for change in Darfur. "When somebody comes to your village, kills children, kills women in front of you, is that right?" one of them asked.

Not far from Um Seifa was the sparse town square of Labado—a dry, hot, windy outpost where the SLA's tattered green, blue, and yellow flag flew overhead. We were greeted by six young men, none over the age of thirty, I would guess, and all armed with Kalashnikov rifles. We sat under the shade of the town square's few trees and began listening. Our hour-long talk was punctuated by the occasional appearance of a badly battered flatbed truck with a machine gun mounted on the side. The truck was covered with dirt and someone had crudely marked "SLA" on the side with their finger. Tellingly, the initials for the SLA's Islamic then-ally, the Justice and Equality Movement (JEM), had been painted over on the side of a building overlooking the square. As I learned later, there were real tensions between the SLA and the JEM—tensions that have since turned bloody, with the two groups now rivals. The SLA does not claim a religious identity; the JEM, however, is an overtly Islamic organization. It is said to have ties to Hassan al-Turabi, the charismatic Islamic leader who was largely responsible for Sudan's "Islamic revival" of the 1980s and 1990s. Since then, however, he has become *persona non grata* with the Sudanese government.

The stories the young men told us had a familiar ring: they could have been uttered by the guerrilla fighters of China, Vietnam, and Latin America in the last century. Coming from humble backgrounds in forgotten places, they had gone to the big city—in this case, Khartoum—to obtain their education. Eventually, after experiencing what they called the heavy hand of discrimination, they joined a guerrilla movement. In this instance, they claimed the prejudice they experienced was due to being "African"—specifically as members of the Zaghawa tribe. "We are African citizens here in Darfur," said one of the young men, age twenty-seven. Although all of the men had lost relatives in the acts of violence in Darfur, their anger and frustration with the government in Khartoum predated the formation of the SLA in 2003. It is difficult, one said, for Darfuris to get jobs in the government. "If you are colored black, you cannot be a government worker," he said.

This neglect of Darfur is true enough—government social spending in Darfur has long lagged behind the rest of Sudan, itself not a bellwether of social progress or equity within Africa. (Sudan is one of the poorest and least developed countries on the planet, according to the United Nations Development Program's Human Development Index.) Darfur's status as a backwater area has a long history, with the western region of Sudan barely registering concern from either the British colonial government or its successors. Gerard Prunier notes that during the 1950s, Sudan had only eighteen maternity clinics—not a single one was in Darfur. Out of twenty-three intermediate schools in Sudan operating in 1952, only one was in Darfur. A check of the library catalogs of both Yale and Columbia universities in the summer of 2008 found few published studies about Darfur written before the current crisis and those about Sudan generally tend to slight Darfur—though there is an explosion of material about Darfur after 2004. A 1959 history, *The Independent Sudan*, by Mekki Shibeika, a historian who taught at the University of Khartoum, does not even index Darfur. The letters of Sir Douglas Newbold, the one-time British civil secretary in Sudan, mention Darfur only in passing.

Given that legacy of neglect, it was not surprising that several of the SLA men explained that they had been involved in protests as students in Khartoum, and had received short prison terms for writing petitions about Darfur. This prompted the men to join the fledgling SLA. While the group says it is dedicated to equality and justice, it pointedly does not call for separation from greater Sudan itself. The SLA's vision is for a united Sudan; their armed rebellion is a last resort of sorts. "We never wanted war," one said. "We are ready for peace." But they doubted that the Sudanese government was committed to what they sought. We pressed them: what do you want? "The land should be for all of us....We want our rights." Did that mean that they believed the land was being taken away from them? To some extent, yes, they answered. They felt that "Arab" nomadic people were "invading" Darfur and taking away land they believed was justly theirs.

Just then, Ramhadan Faber Adam, a leader of the SLA's Labado front, arrived in the town square. We subsequently learned that Adam was involved in the on-again, off-again peace negotiations with Khartoum. It was immediately clear from his magisterial bearing and the deference shown by his men that all questions were now to be directed to him. His manner was clipped and often cold. Commander Adam dismissed a question about the SLA's philosophy as if he were swatting a fly: "I don't understand your metaphysics," he snapped. We asked about his impressions of the *Janjaweed* militias. Given the angry tone we heard earlier from his troops, we were caught off guard by his response. "We don't have a problem with the *Janjaweed*," he said. "They are pawns. Those who are behind the *Janjaweed*—they are the ones who concern us." We asked him the same question we asked his men: what exactly were the SLA's motives? "Justice, equality, sharing of wealth," he said. "We are not getting anything from the government."

What of the peace agreement then being negotiated between the Khartoum government and southern Sudan? Would it have any bearing on the Darfur situation? He seemed a bit piqued and responded coldly: "They have their problems; we have our problems. Peace in the south will not bring a solution to the problems in Darfur." We tried to press him further, but he cut us off. "It's not linked to us. In the south, the government of Sudan used religion and ethnicity as tools. Here they are using tribal conflicts." Then he smiled. "We are happy we are fighting. We started a war where and when we wanted." This issue of war and peace was perhaps the murkiest of all the topics we discussed: the young men felt war was something that had been pushed on them. But Adam's proud boasting sounded like the bravado of a commander trying to impress a group of visitors.

We were not the first to get the "SLA treatment." In late 2004, one SLA fighter suggested to *Washington Post* reporter Emily Wax that if the group had five hundred vehicles mounted with machine guns, it could "take Khartoum in a month." Like us, Wax was not easily impressed. After spending a week with the guerillas, she wrote that the SLA was "an ill-equipped, untrained and disorganized group, with child fighters among its ranks. Its grand ambitions are not matched by its resources. The only thing the rebels don't seem to be lacking is motivation." Still, this ragtag army *had* shaken the Sudanese government to its very core. Alex de Waal notes that by attacking a Darfur airport, destroying military aircraft, and kidnapping an air force general, the SLA managed to pull off what the Sudanese Peoples' Liberation Army (SPLA), the rebel group that fought the Khartoum government in southern Sudan, had not been able to accomplish in some twenty years of fighting. The SLA rebels in Darfur, de Waal notes, "had mobility, good intelligence and popular support." The rebels' action, the resulting government counterinsurgency, and the international reaction to the crisis in Darfur amounted to a convulsion that represented "a more profound challenge to the government's legitimacy than the war in the south ever did." (JEM also had its successes: on May 10, 2008, JEM rebels got as far as heavily fortified Khartoum, eliciting outcries by

President al-Bashir that neighboring Chad was behind the attack.)

While Adam and his men could appear formidable, what we later saw in the area patrolled by the young SLA guerrillas we initially met was worrisome. They worked at the roadside by night, checking identification of those on buses and trucks driving through the area, and as schoolteachers and administrators by day. We were given a tour of the small community where they performed their dual roles of teachers and SLA commandos with a mixture of aplomb and grim seriousness. Muhammad Haru Musa, twenty-seven, the young school principal, seemed to be goading his charges into saying favorable things about the SLA. Like Muhammad and his associates, the children had lost family members to attacks by the *Janjaweed* and the government. One fourteen-year-old student piped up, "When I grow up, I'll join the movement." Why? "To defend my family and community."

Some, even younger, did not need goading. As we left this area the next day, we saw youngsters not much older than the boy who spoke in class with Kalashnikov rifles strung around their shoulders. We couldn't be sure they were SLA child soldiers who had seen battle. But we also couldn't be sure that they were mere mascots or hangers-on. It was hard not to gawk.

✦   ✦   ✦

In the village of Um Seifa, away from the blaze of Darfur's midday heat, in cool star-filled nights, or in the soft light of mornings, it was possible to catch a glimpse of what life might be like without war: dogs barking and cattle quietly stirring; mothers feeding their infants and preparing their older children for school. But just days after I left Darfur in December 2004, Um Seifa and the surrounding area, including Labado, was attacked, causing dozens of women and children to flee in terror. One of my colleagues wrote to me, "That's a place in the world which is no longer there." Given our encounter with the SLA, the news didn't really come as a surprise. This was an area controlled by the rebel groups. My colleague, who had worked in southern Sudan for years, was no stranger to the government Antonov bomber we saw late one afternoon as we hurriedly left the zone for fear of attack. Nonetheless, there was an element of shock: we knew this place, even for just a few days.

✦   ✦   ✦

The Labeling Debate

In 2004, while the world debated what to call the Darfur crisis—genocide, ethnic cleansing, a counterinsurgency that got out of hand—in Darfur itself, the labeling often did not seem to matter. This was "a dirty war" in which civilians, not soldiers, bore the brunt of violence. The anthropologist Carolyn Nordstrom has written that in this type of war, with its attendant casualties and death, its devastation of everyday life, its landscapes "full of burned-out villages, maimed people, and families mourning their dead," those who have experienced these horrors hold only "an anti-atrocity ideology." People merely want to survive.

Among the survivors was Adam Ali, a thirty-four-year-old man I met in an SLA-held area. Weeks before I met Ali, he had been shot and wounded, as had fifty-seven-year-old Faddallah Mohammed Harif, an elderly man by Darfur standards. Both men had fled a camp where twelve other people had been killed; the two men were on their way to look for food and water. I am not sure how Harif fled because he had the thinnest legs I have seen on an adult: the width of brittle tree branches. Not far from the two men, next to a lean-to covered with plastic sheeting to protect against the piercing afternoon sun and heat, sat Radija Adam Amhed, a twenty-year-old woman with six children by her side. Her family was waiting for the return of her husband, the children's father, who had gone to fetch water. Displaced twice and looking for safety, Amhed was not sure where the family would eventually land. At the moment we saw her, she was preoccupied with the needs of her sick children, who were suffering from diarrhea. "We have so many problems," she said quietly.

A Scandinavian colleague and I had no food or medicine with us. There was nothing we could marshal except tepid words of support. It was one of those discouraging moments when the work of a writer is often inadequate in the face of dire need. But the encounter prompted my friend to say the need for civilian protection—"protection, protection, protection," he would repeat—was the greatest need in Darfur. My colleague was not alone. It was a mantra I would hear repeatedly in my remaining weeks in Darfur. By 2004, humanitarian personnel in Darfur were obsessed with a desire to protect civilians from further violence. To those working in Darfur, the parallel international debate on genocide was important but also felt like something terribly distant. In the wake of post–September 11 international politics, the genocide debate had become overly politicized, they argued. One humanitarian worker from Great Britain emphatically warned, "If it's politicized, stay away from it." What she meant was that the genocide debate was now inseparable from other issues related to global politics (such as the U.S.-led Iraq war) and that too much time had been spent trying to define what was happening in Darfur and not enough was being done to stop it.

Discussing the "g-word," as it was often called among humanitarians in Darfur, was a tricky matter among relief workers, who care deeply about human rights but are keenly aware of how debates over genocide in Darfur affected their work. There were decided shades of gray—one reason being that humanitarian and human rights workers have parallel but slightly dissimilar missions. While the humanitarians provide basic materials for survival (food, medicine, and the like), human rights workers investigate abuses and advocate on behalf of survivors. They are like cousins: you can see the family resemblance, but you can also see there are clear differences, and possibilities for problems and disagreements. In a sense, humanitarian workers labor on the inside, while human rights investigators operate on the outside. By necessity, humanitarian personnel are careful, no matter how they might feel about a government, to foster a working relationship with local authorities. By contrast, human rights workers are like investigative reporters; their evaluations are meant to cast a light on abuses under way.

Over tea during a work break in one of the humanitarian compounds, a European humanitarian worker—who, like many others, is not being named because of the fear of reprisal or the very real possibility of being asked to leave Sudan—cautiously ventured that the use of the term "genocide" in the context of Darfur *had* become too politicized. The word "required a very high threshold of proof," she said. "If we value the term, we have to treat it very carefully." She paused for a moment, choosing her words deliberately. "If we have failed in Darfur and it is genocide, that will be enormously sad," she said. "I don't know if it's genocide or not. But I've worked in a lot of post-conflict places—Iraq, Afghanistan—and this is the most suffering I've ever seen." Another woman pointedly and repeatedly asked about "intent," a key provision of the Convention on the Prevention and Punishment of Genocide. Intent, she claimed, was still not clear, nor was what she called "the Darfur endgame."

"Was it the deliberate destruction of the Fur people?" she asked, referring to one of the largest ethnic groups in Darfur. "In a technical sense," she said, what had happened seemed "to point to that." But at the same time, she noted, the term genocide had become overused and popularized. To a public used to hazy references over issues of history and international law, the differences between a Darfur and a Rwanda were becoming less distinct.

The most passionate—certainly the most impatient—humanitarian was a European United Nations worker who claimed he did not care what the Darfur crisis was called. "I don't think labeling anything has been helpful at all," he said one afternoon in his small office. "Discussing semantics has wasted time; stopping the violence should be the principal objective." He found the debate over genocide altogether maddening. He pointed out that no one had yet determined how to protect those in the camps—there were still too few African Union peacekeepers and their mandate was severely limited. The assaults against civilians in the camps were reduced when outside humanitarian workers were present, but there were too few workers to make any real difference. Citing a time in November 2004 when the BBC taped incidents of harassment within Kalma, the largest displacement camp in Darfur, he asked, "What's protection by presence if a

Kalma happens? Kalma is the most protected place there is, but in the end there's not really that much protection at all. 'Protection by presence' becomes nothing but an empty phrase."

By implication, the UN worker was suggesting, rightly in retrospect, that too much was being expected of humanitarian groups. Too many people faced violence, and precious little could be done by overstretched humanitarian workers who themselves faced threats, government harassment, and numerous bureaucratic obstacles. Given these problems and the fact that a political solution had not been found, there was an unsettling feeling that the aid efforts themselves were contributing to the status quo. An official of the relief agency Doctors Without Borders told *New York Times* columnist Nicholas Kristof, in effect, "the aid effort is sustaining victims so they can be killed with a full belly."

At least one other idea was discussed by Darfuris in the camps. For some of them, the solution seemed relatively easy: send in outside protection forces, preferably from the West. Many distrusted the motives of other African countries. In the recent tangled history of Sudan, Eritrea is seen as an enemy by some, Chad by others. One man wanted an even more radical gesture: he said he wanted the United States to intervene *militarily* and actually fight the *Janjaweed* in hand-to-hand combat. I didn't have the heart to tell him that I doubted that would ever happen. The United States was preoccupied by a war in another predominately Muslim country. Besides, the international community had failed to act in Rwanda. A decade later, the world still had no consensus about how or when to intervene in places like Darfur.

Why hadn't it? Writer David Rieff, a trenchant critic of the ways humanitarianism can go awry, has suggested that in matters like Darfur, "Good will is not enough; nor is political will."

> That is because, as Iraq has taught us so painfully, the law of unintended consequences may be one of the few iron laws of international politics. And somewhere, despite all the outcry, leaders know that the same people calling for intervention may repudiate it the moment it goes wrong.

Sadly, when I returned to Darfur in 2007, the world was still leaving the problem up to humanitarian groups. Some non-African aid workers argued not enough time had been spent on a comprehensive peace agreement that could address crucial social and humanitarian questions. The high-profile debates, from their perspective, had done little to save lives in Darfur. It was different for some African workers, who either said nothing or quietly suggested that the genocide question *was* important. I pulled aside an African worker in 2007 and asked him what he thought about the genocide question. He appeared to ignore it. In another instance, one Western aid official working in Darfur expressed some frustration over the genocide debate, saying he did not think a legal "threshold" for genocide had been exceeded, or even reached, in Darfur. After a Sudanese aid worker heard this, she told a colleague of mine, "For us, it *is* genocide."

"Hens in Cages"

Upon my return in 2007, the best evidence of any tangible progress was found in the camps themselves. There was a mixture of change and permanence. One change had nothing to do with the crisis: I visited in early September, at the end of the rainy season—the parched, brittle landscape of December had become sodden, verdant countryside. Roads were muddy and sometimes impassable. In the city center of Zalingei in West Darfur stood massive pieces of pipe—part of an uncompleted water drainage system—embedded in mud and water. The green of September made Darfur seem more hospitable, but the rains also contributed to seasonal upturns in disease and illness, heightening the complaints of those in the displacement camps. One of the camps I had gotten to know was remarkably the same: idleness and a sense of weariness, particularly among young men, still seemed to grip the place. There remained just a single clinic and dispensary for a population of more than fifty thousand persons. The camp still looked and smelled as if it were a potential firetrap, with thorn branches serving as fencing just feet away from open stoves. It still felt crowded. Once again I heard residents compare their lives to those of "hens in cages."

"We had a beautiful life," said one woman, recalling the rhythms of fetching water, raising cattle and vegetables, and the pleasures of enjoying milk and beef in a meal. "We never dreamed that criminals would take this away from us." That comment was telling—and in one sense welcome: first, because it named criminal acts and second, because it came from a woman.

When I visited in 2004, it was nearly impossible for a white male from the United States to speak to women in the camps, not only about the sensitive subject of rape and sexual assault, but about anything substantial. I had to speak discreetly to tribal leaders who knew the women. This was frustrating—the men themselves used euphemisms to describe the women's situation. The issue of rape and violent assaults was the most obvious and most sensitive.

By contrast, even taking into account gaps of culture and sensitivity about trauma and rape, the women in 2007 appeared far more confident. They had organized into groups, and were not shy about giving themselves a collective identity as survivors of rape and displacement. They cheered support for Abdul Wahid Mohammad al-Nur, an SLA founder, and a conspicuous holdout among participants in Darfur peace talks. Nur argued that peace negotiations could not take place until there is greater security in Darfur. His militancy had made him a hero among the displaced, and seemed to point to increasing support for the rebel cause among those stuck in the camps for years.

If there was a face to this new development, it was Fatima Adam (no relation to the SLA's Commander Ramhadan Faber Adam), a formidable, blunt, and outspoken woman. Adam was not afraid to spell out a litany of grievances about camp conditions to a group of visitors from U.S. and European church-based humanitarian groups. She included the still lamentable but never-resolved fear of being assaulted or raped as the women gathered firewood outside of the camps. Apparently attempts to have the men do this type of "women's work" went nowhere. "The needs are still great," Adam told us. She waved her fist as she declared the need for the United Nations peacekeeping force to protect those in the camps. "We're tired of living in this prison."

The prison analogy evoked by Adam and others was more poignant in 2007 than in 2004. Many of them had been in the camp for three, even four years. It actually *had* become a prison—or maybe even worse: at least in prison there is the hope of a release date. Moreover, a prisoner about to be paroled knows there is a structured society on the outside. By 2007, no such guarantees existed in Darfur. A new wave of displacement, some fifty-five thousand people, had occurred in the months before I arrived. This displacement was not merely due to the familiar pattern of strikes by government militias and the *Janjaweed*—though such attacks would start to mount again in late 2007. Rather, it was due to inter- and intraethnic violence among and between split-away factions of rebels and the government-aligned militia. Feuding factions were trying to gain control of areas before the "hybrid" force of United Nations and African Union peacekeepers arrived in early 2008. This prompted the dry, understated use of the word "fluid"—as in the "security situation is fluid" (which nearly always means "out of control"). Here the word really meant something: whereas once there were two rebel factions, there were by then as many as two dozen or more—a veritable "hodgepodge of groups," said one observer of a situation in which *Janjaweed* fighters had joined the rebel forces they once fought. Some were angry that they were owed payment for their work with the military units; they now sought protection money in areas they once raided.

"The fact is, we don't really know what's going on," said one exasperated official. Another worker, a young Ugandan engineer, told me over a dinner of goat and okra that "this situation or something like it could still exist ten years from now." Before dinner, the engineer showed me his work—a well in a camp that clearly was good for the camp residents. They were enjoying fresh water, and women did not have to gather it under the threat of attack. He was proud of the well. But the engineer and other humanitarian workers knew that their aid could only go so far. "Without a peace agreement," another worker told me, pointing to rows and rows of tents, "this is what you'll get."

❖   ❖   ❖

Two memories from 2007: I attended an obligatory meeting of two officials of Sudan's Humanitarian Affairs Commission (HAC) in the same dank, dark, water-stained office in Zalingei I had visited three years earlier. Sitting at a desk adorned with a box of tissues and an open tin of cookies, one of the men wore faux leopard slippers as he praised the work of the humanitarian groups in the camps. "Highly appreciated," he said, adding, though, it was ultimately up to the Sudanese government and authorities like him to provide "peace and security" for the displaced.

His colleague—a commanding, gray-haired man—also tried to cast conditions in an optimistic light but through an entirely different set of lenses. He declared there was no tension between the displaced people in the camps and people in the large towns or cities of Darfur. This is not true in Darfur camps and rarely true anywhere where displaced people find themselves next to an established population center—those established in the town often resent the presence of outsiders. Moreover, he claimed that the displaced people had filled an employment gap in Zalingei. "We have a larger labor force now," he said, as if poor, muddy, battered Zalingei was a tech mecca in need of skilled workers.

The second memory: returning to Khartoum, flying out of the airport in Nyala. Under overcast skies laden with drizzle, the region's stalemates seemed to be symbolically played out on the tarmac. There, as if facing each other in a standoff, stood commercial aircraft, Sudanese military fighter jets, African Union helicopters, and UN humanitarian transport planes.

All sat motionless.

CHAPTER

3

Sounding the Alarm

(Whoever) passively accepts evil is as much involved in it as (the person) who helps to perpetuate it. (Whoever) accepts evil without protesting against it is really cooperating with it.

— Martin Luther King Jr., *Stride Toward Freedom* (1958)

If planes standing still symbolized Darfur in the summer of 2007, an odder symbol emerged a year later: within days of the International Criminal Court's request for the arrest of President al-Bashir, the president set out for Darfur, waving a cane and dancing a jig atop a flatbed truck. It was hard to tell from the outside precisely what this public display meant. One colleague told me the behavior was unseemly, even unsettling, "like Hitler touring the death camps"—a *génocidaire* visiting the scene of the crime, as it were. Was it an act of defiance against the West, given the grudges Sudan's leaders still nurse from the colonial past? Could it be political theater aimed at a domestic audience? Or was it simply a man running scared? U.S. Darfur activists were not as troubled as my colleague was about this display. They had greeted the ICC action as a substantial achievement, and also hoped that a cornered al-Bashir might, at last, be compelled to do something positive in Darfur. After all, the initial worries that al-Bashir's government might act rashly in the wake of the indictment—by taking aim at humanitarian workers and forcing agencies out, or cracking down anew—had not occurred. "The Nazis did this type of thing—they put on plays, opened up camps to the Red Cross," said Mark Hanis, one of the founders of the Genocide Intervention Network, a grassroots organization. "It's not unusual for them to put on a show; it makes sense. He's under attack, so he changes the focus." Hanis's colleague, Chad Hazlett, said that given the other alternatives—a feared "doomsday scenario" of a full-out government crackdown on aid agencies—the sight of Bashir making jolly around Darfur was not the worst thing that could happen.

Human rights activist John Prendergast agreed. As cochair of the antigenocide initiative the ENOUGH Project, he was happy with the ICC action, calling the al-Bashir publicity tour a "short-term defiance," which probably masked some real fright; it was likely, he said, that the al-Bashir government could "see the handwriting on the wall." He added, "They can't take this lightly. They are not the Taliban or Sadaam Hussein: they want to be accepted by the international community, to be an actor on the world stage." He said the government had been smart "not to go on a full frontal assault; they've played their cards well. Good for them; they're playing the game." Prendergast viewed the action as a vindication for activists who had sought serious sanction for action in Darfur. He described the ICC's decision as an "incredible tool" of leverage by the international community. He did not believe, however, the arrest warrant itself amounted to a full success, saying that would only come when a peace agreement was reached. Until then, the government of Sudan could continue to act in ways it had long mastered: obfuscation, impeding humanitarian groups, and slowing any efforts toward a peace settlement. "This is still a pretty serious humanitarian emergency that is brewing," Prendergast cautioned, "and the government of Sudan still has all sorts of tools it can use, rather than performing an all-out assault."

Small Victory Amid Frustrations

When the ICC decision finally came, it gave the activist community a much-needed boost. For several years, activist efforts to pressure the Khartoum government to change its ways or Western governments to act on Darfur had been frustrated. In the spring of 2005, Canadian General and Senator Roméo Dallaire, a fellow at Harvard University's Carr Center for Human Rights Policy and an eyewitness to the Rwandan genocide, noted that the Khartoum government "was making the international community dance to *its* tune."

How and precisely why this happened, at least in relation to the United States, will be debated by historians. This much we do know: in a fine summary of U.S. policy over Darfur that appeared in October 2007, *Washington Post* reporter Michael Abramowitz wrote that President George W. Bush himself expressed an unusual amount of passion on the issue of Darfur. The president told a group of Darfur activists that he felt that the *Janjaweed* needed to be brought to justice and what had happened in Darfur *was* genocide. In fact, the extent of Bush's passion caused some of his staff to dub him the "Sudan desk officer." But others within the Bush administration said the president had "not matched his words with action, allowing initiatives to drop because of inertia or failure to follow up, while proving unable to mobilize either his bureaucracy or the international community," according to the *Post*.

Abramowitz's report continued: "The president who famously promised not to allow another Rwanda mass murder on his watch has never fully chosen between those inside his government advocating more pressure on Sudan and those advocating engagement with its Islamist government, so the policy has veered from one approach to another."

According to Abramowitz, the administration had grappled with how, exactly, outsiders could provide security for the displaced in Darfur, but always came up against intractable dilemmas:

> While almost everyone involved in Darfur policy agrees that an African Union peacekeeping force of just 7,000 troops is not up to the task, the United States has refused to send troops and, despite promises of reinforcements, has yet to secure many additional troops from other countries. At the same time, it has been unable to broker a diplomatic resolution that might ease the violence.

> Even Bush has complained privately that his hands are tied on Darfur because, with the U.S. involvement in Iraq and Afghanistan he cannot be seen as "invading another Muslim country," according to people who have spoken with him about the issue.

> "It's impossible to keep Iraq out of this picture," said Edward Mortimer, who served as a top aide to then-U.N. Secretary-General Kofi Annan and says resentment over Iraq caused many countries to not want to cooperate with the United States on Darfur.

To be fair to the United States, the Abramowitz report noted, other problems pressed in as well: "the limitations of working through institutions such as the United Nations, NATO, and the African Union. They (administration officials) cite the billions of dollars of U.S. relief aid that has kept millions of Sudanese alive. They say U.S. pressure has kept the issue on the world's agenda." The report continued:

> "If there was ever a case study where the president sees the limitation and frustrations of the multilateral organizations, it is the issue of Darfur," said Dan Bartlett, former White House counselor. "Everybody for the most part can come to a consensus: Whether you call it genocide or not, we have an urgent security and humanitarian crisis on our hands. Yet these institutions cannot garner the will or ability to come together to save people."

> There is no doubt that responsibility for inaction on Darfur can be spread around. The Sudanese government has resisted cooperation at every step in the saga and has been shielded at the United Nations by China, its main international protector.

The report also noted that with the "notable exception of Britain and some Nordic countries," few other countries expressed much interest or concern about Darfur. "There's an enormous stain on the world's conscience," said Mitchell B. Reiss, former State Department policy planning chief. "We collectively stood by and let it happen a decade after it happened in Rwanda." Interestingly, the report notes that in 2005, Bush contemplated military action in Darfur. "He wanted to go in and kill the *Janjaweed*," said one advisor quoted by *The Washington Post*. But "people had to restrain him." When aides warned him of the risks of getting "involved in another shooting war . . . the president backed off."

It is hard to read this report and believe that inaction on Darfur was simply due to timidity. In fact, there *were* U.S. policy dilemmas, not easily solved, many of them due to the fact that the United States was fighting a war in Iraq. Yet the issue was also an *international* problem: the permanent members of the UN Security Council all had ties to Khartoum that were hard to shake. China, with its growing export market for goods in Sudan and its burgeoning investment in oil there, was the most obvious example. There were others: Russia and France had long sold military aircraft and weaponry to Sudan. Great Britain, Sudan's one-time colonial ruler, was not in a position to say much about Darfur given that it too had military forces in Iraq. Moreover, ties between the United States and Sudan, while never very good, improved after the events of September 11, 2001. The United States found itself closer to Khartoum because the government of Sudan could provide much-needed intelligence information, though there was never unanimity within the U.S. government about whether that was a wise move.

In fact, as a June 2005 report in the *Los Angeles Times* noted, a heated debate and split among government officials ensued about a CIA decision to fly Major General Salah Abdallah Gosh, the Sudanese government's intelligence chief, to the United States for secret meetings in April 2005. The *Times* described these meetings as "cementing cooperation against terrorism." The report quoted a congressional researcher as saying that Gosh's sanctioned visit would "send a political signal to the [Sudanese] government that Darfur would not prevent Sudan from winning support in Washington." The trip was justified by one official quoted by the *Times* given that Gosh "has strategic knowledge and information about a critical region in the war on terror." But the visit angered members of the Congressional Black Caucus, and prompted Representative Donald M. Payne, a New Jersey Democrat, to declare that the Gosh visit was "tantamount to inviting the head of the Nazi SS at the height of the Holocaust."

It is difficult to predict how Barack Obama's administration will deal with the Darfur crisis given the host of domestic and international problems the new president faces. During the 2008 presidential campaign, Obama said that as president he would take "immediate steps to end the genocide in Darfur" by increasing pressure on the Sudanese government "to halt the killing and stop impeding the deployment of a robust inter-national force." At the same time, his campaign aides told *The New York Times* that if elected, Obama would probably be reluctant to send U.S. troops to Darfur given U.S. commitments in Afghanistan and Iraq. Even so, Susan E. Rice, Obama's long-time foreign policy advisor and the incoming U.S. ambassador to the United Nations, has advocated the possible need for military action to stop acts of genocide.

◆   ◆   ◆

The haphazard and incoherent nature of Sudan's realities are quickly apparent and grasped. My first interview in 2004 proved prescient in many ways. While still in the capital of Khartoum and before arriving in Darfur, I interviewed a European development worker. This man was passionate. He spoke with a clear love for the Sudanese people and a clear frustration for what he saw developing in Darfur.

He was my first guide to Sudan's political landscape and my notes mirror his scattershot way of excitedly moving from one topic to the next. Still, four years after our meeting, much, maybe even most, of what he said still seems to hold—a damning snapshot about how little had changed between 2004 and 2008.

Call this, then, "Nine Suppositions on Darfur."

(1) He criticized humanitarian aid operations for making people dependent on relief assistance. "There's no sustainable development where people live," he said of village life. "Think of a woman in Darfur; in the camp, she has health care and water; her life is better now than it was. Of course, she's going to the camp; she doesn't have to fetch water for two hours." (In hindsight this is only partly true: women face continued dangers of threat and sexual assault in the camps. It's a contradiction of sorts, but contradictions are part of the Darfur narrative.)

(2) He described the displacement camps as prisons where it was too small to even have a garden. (I discovered later that's not quite true, although those in the camps are quite frustrated by the small size of the plots they are able to cultivate.)

(3) "It's evil; it's a disaster."

(4) There is no political will for a military intervention in Darfur and for obvious, "real-politik" reasons: "The French do not want to alienate the Arab world; the United States and the UK have Iraq to deal with and can't afford any extra problems; Russia trades arms with Sudan; China wants Sudan's oil." The bottom line: "Nobody wants to pay for peace in Sudan."

(5) He warned that other areas of the country are falling into chaos, saying, "Darfur is one of many conflicts in Sudan. Other conflicts are possible."

(6) "Darfur showed the real heart of this government."

(7) The Sudanese government started something over which it has no control; as the situation spirals, the government can't stop it. "In a 'shame culture' like this, they don't want to say: 'We don't have control.'"

(8) African Union peacekeeping forces are not only poorly trained and poorly organized, "the AU is the cover for the West to do nothing."

(9) "Sudan, not just Darfur, is a lost cause."

❖   ❖   ❖

A Global Responsibility to Protect

Was Darfur a lost cause? The dilemmas of the Darfur tragedy quickly became the province of academic study, particularly as political theorists dealt with the fallout of the notion of humanitarian intervention, a term that arose in the 1990s during the crises of Rwanda and the Balkans. David Rieff has called humanitarian intervention "at once an immensely powerful and a terribly imprecise idea. No formal legal definition of it exists, but its fundamental premise is that outside powers have the right and, perhaps, under some circumstances, the duty to intervene to protect people in other countries who are being victimized, even if what is taking place is a conflict within a state."

During a spring 2005 sabbatical at Harvard Divinity School, I attended a class at Harvard's John F. Kennedy School of Government taught by an expert who has written extensively on the dilemmas posed by humanitarian intervention. Writer and political theorist Michael Ignatieff subsequently left Harvard to return to his native Canada and launch a successful campaign for a seat in the Canadian Parliament. A long-time human rights advocate and a tough, engaged, probing questioner of students, Ignatieff possessed a sense of tragedy to help students understand that none of the decisions about Darfur could possibly be easy. Indeed, the slightly elegiac mood of the class might have been due to Ignatieff's public declarations on the Iraq war. Ignatieff had supported the war in Iraq on human rights grounds, but later concluded that the war had been a mistake. (This did not stop some critics, such as British author and activist Richard Seymour, from criticizing Ignatieff as an apologist for empire.) Ignatieff told the class of future policymakers, diplomats, and military leaders that there is ultimately a "commonsense threshold" to pass: "Can you walk up to a family that has lost a son or daughter and say, 'This was just and here's why.' If you can't do that, don't do it."

The underlying foundation to Ignatieff's class was this: there has been a human rights revolution in recent decades—something welcome and helpful but also problematic. The "ground zero" of human rights is a sense of global equality—what some call "cosmopolitanism," the idea that all in the world have a place within a shared moral community. In this vision, Africans are just as important as Americans. But in an imperfect, tragic world, there are choices to be made: to whom do we owe protection? Universal human rights have not generated universal obligations. To a U.S. citizen, the life of a fellow U.S. citizen is likely to matter more than a Somali life. "It's not saying that Somali lives are less valuable than U.S. lives," Ignatieff said, using the example of Somalia. "Somalis matter—they will grieve the way you grieve." But if you are a U.S. policymaker considering sending U.S. troops to, say, Darfur—you have to ask if the United States has a duty to help solve what is, at base, a Sudanese problem.

The human rights revolution had, at least in theory, changed the well-established idea that the sovereignty of states was inviolate. But the idea of sovereignty has now changed: states now have a moral responsibility to protect those living within its borders. An April 2006 United Nations Security Council resolution that affirms a declaration made at the 2005 World Summit says each individual state "has the responsibility to protect its populations from genocide, war crimes, ethnic cleansing and crimes against humanity." This responsibility, the UN declares, "entails the prevention of such crimes, including their incitement, through appropriate and necessary means." The resolution also affirms a declaration that the international community, "through the United Nations, also has the responsibility to use appropriate diplomatic, humanitarian and other peaceful means . . . to help protect populations from genocide, war crimes, ethnic cleansing and crimes against humanity."

What "protection" means is not precisely clear. This new notion of the "responsibility to protect" is at odds with the older idea of sovereign states that could, international condemnation and opprobrium aside, pretty much do as they pleased. Adding to this complicated mix, as Ignatieff described it, is the idea that states that "manifestly fail" to protect their citizens cease to be "legitimate within the international system." A Sudanese taxi driver put it to me very simply: "That's not right, what al-Bashir is doing. A government is supposed to protect you; not *kill* you."

If sovereign states do not provide protection, then it is up to the international community to intervene and offer it. But the *how* remains unresolved. Former colonial countries in Africa and Asia are worried that the "responsibility to protect" is just another example of what they perceive as European or U.S. dominance over continents like Africa. Ignatieff's answer to that: there needs to be *less* intervention, not *more*. Nations should be strengthened and empowered as "agents of moral duty" to protect their citizens. Of course, given the human rights record of the Sudanese government, that was not likely to happen.

So the specific question about Darfur remained: what to do? Ignatieff argued this question could not be answered until others were resolved. Perhaps the most central (and still contested) question was simply how to characterize the conflict: was Darfur genocide? Ethnic cleansing? A counterinsurgency out of control? It was not enough, he said, for a policymaker to say civilians were attacked and innocent blood was shed. Admittedly, the term "innocent civilians" was probably more applicable in Darfur than just about anywhere else in the last twenty years. Yet Darfur *was* also the site of an insurgency, and that changed the equation. Moreover, opting to intervene in Darfur might affect the peace process in that part of the country but bring trouble to other areas.

The questions and dilemmas continued. There was the issue of deniability—something "always structured into genocide," Ignatieff said. The *Janjaweed* were used as surrogates, so it could always be argued that the *Janjaweed* were a force unto themselves. Another challenge was to resolve one of the root causes of conflict: tensions between Darfur's farmers and nomads.

At nearly every turn, interventionists in Darfur face the problems of destabilizing consequences, Ignatieff argued. There was the issue of civilian protection versus remaining neutral: how could this be done? Ring the camps? If so, with troops? Humanitarian workers? Peacekeepers? What about the *Janjaweed*? As soon as an intervening group repelled them militarily, neutrality would be lost. How does anyone protect civilians, remain neutral, take on the *Janjaweed*, and not be drawn into a battle with both the *Janjaweed* and the Sudanese army? How could the situation be stabilized for the internally displaced without making them permanently displaced? "The protection issue is a nightmare," he concluded.

Looking toward the future, Ignatieff argued, the problems of Darfur could only be solved by a combination of political, military/protection, and humanitarian action. His vision of a humanitarian response was not "just feeding," but a "development strategy to resolve the conflicts caused by changing environmental problems and the nomad/pastoralist tensions." All of this was complicated by the fact that "Khartoum has passed the cost of protection to the international community and that created a perverse effect." Darfur had become a ward of the international community and a humanitarian problem that the Khartoum government had forced on the rest of the world. "Ruthless leaders pass on their oppression internationally," he said of situations like Darfur, "and we get suckered into doing their dirty work."

Ignatieff remarked with a mixture of quiet resignation, irony, and exasperation that "there is no limit to the moral ingenuity of states" like Sudan in working around situations like Darfur.

Was it any wonder, then, that al-Bashir danced as he did?

Darfur: An Insolvable Problem?

If it was Michael Ignatieff's job to relay a much-needed sense of limits and caution to future policymakers studying at Harvard, it was Samantha Power's task to keep the fires of idealism burning in those who might serve in government or nongovernmental organizations. Power is notably adept at juggling the roles of activist, scholar, journalist, and policy advisor to Barack Obama. Power's *A Problem from Hell: America and the Age of Genocide* examined the history of the usually laggard response of the United States to genocide during the twentieth century and became a seminal text for those concerned about Darfur. Power's presence at Harvard was probably one reason that the university became a center for Darfur activism. Student activists were credited with pushing the university in the spring of 2005 to become the first major educational institution to divest from companies doing business in Sudan. Throughout that spring semester, Darfur forums were numerous, attended by Harvard students who, like Power, wore the ubiquitous green "Not on Our Watch" wristbands. An oft-repeated slogan was taken from an April 2004 op-ed piece Power wrote for the *New York Times* marking the tenth anniversary of the Rwandan genocide: "Remember Rwanda but Take Action in Sudan."

When teaching her class on U.S. foreign policy and human rights in 2005, Power was less an activist and more a thorough analyst. Power noted with pride that Bush and his first secretary of state, Colin Powell, both labeled Darfur as "genocide" while it occurred—a first in U.S. history. (The Clinton administration had not done the same while the Rwanda genocide unfolded.) This was due, she argued, to an impressive domestic constituency that had become passionate about the issue. While some of this—maybe even much of it—was due to guilt over Rwanda, Power felt the degree of engagement by activists, particularly students, was striking and welcome. "Almost nothing that has happened about Darfur has come from the top down, but from grassroots activism," she said to students as the semester drew to a close. "We should feel good about what we've accomplished. But we can't lose sight of the fact that three hundred thousand people have died." She said Darfur could very well "morph into one of these impossible, insolvable problems." Darfur had come to matter to people but in the ways of hard lessons learned—that good intentions are not, never are, and never will be, good enough. "The clock is ticking for the people of Darfur."

I spoke to Power before I finished my sabbatical. She reiterated the frustration that there was "so much mobilization and bipartisan support on Capitol Hill," and yet the activist community had, for the moment, probably done all it could do. "You have two thousand flowers blooming, but they're blooming in the Sahara—people are dressed up with nowhere to go." Once again, the United States, as well as other countries, was bound "by the constraints of national interests." Such interests—be it China's search for oil or the U.S. need for intelligence—"cut against" the impassioned advocacy and sense of urgency felt by activists. "I'm impressed with what Darfur has brought out in people," she said, adding that, in small ways, "small victories" had sent a message that mobilization could prompt some action. "Maybe we're losing the battle, but strengthening the ranks for the war."

The issue of Darfur has had its champions: in an interesting spot where academia met activism were Power and Eric Reeves, a medieval literature scholar at Smith College who became an impassioned Darfur activist; in the media, columnist Nicholas Kristof of *The New York Times* became known for his sharp reporting and commentary about Darfur, and NBC's Ann Curry tried to keep the issue alive on her network. Among actor-celebrities, George Clooney, Don Cheadle, and Mia Farrow all visited displacement camps, talked to survivors, and used their fame to draw attention to Darfur. (Not everyone was enamored of this dynamic. Writing in the fall 2008 issue of *World Affairs*, Alex de Waal argued against what he called "the moral hyperventilation of celebrities." The people of Darfur, he wrote, "couldn't have asked for more celebrity endorsement. But they still haven't gotten what they need—fighting and suffering continue with no end in sight." Some involved in humanitarian work understand de Waal's critique but also say celebrities are simply filling a void caused by a lack of strong international political leadership.) Brian Steidel, a former U.S. Marine and advisor to African Union forces in Darfur, documented the early stages of the *Janjaweed* and military atrocities and became an impassioned Darfur activist.

Canadian General Roméo Dallaire was a different kind of champion. He had commanded the United Nations peacekeeping forces in Rwanda at the time of the 2004 genocide and had not been able to stop the violence, for which he felt great remorse: he suffered a breakdown when he returned to Canada, feeling he had not done enough. (Others disagreed: Michael Ignatieff introduced Dallaire to his Harvard students by saying, "This man did a lot with inadequate forces.") His guilt prompted Dallaire to make Darfur something of a cause, earning him praise by human rights groups.

Samantha Power described Dallaire as a cult hero to activists and compared him to a "U2 concert." She acknowledged that being a public figure, if not a celebrity of sorts, had exacted a toll. Just when Dallaire was beginning to make peace with himself, the public attention on Rwanda and Darfur made Dallaire relive his trauma. "He'd love to just be the messenger, but he's the message." she added. "He really wants to make a difference, at great personal cost; he knows he is being eaten at; you either choose yourself or the cause… the general is the cause." He has to grapple with the dichotomy of being hailed as a hero, while still feeling like a failure. "It's difficult for him to juxtapose the private guilt and the public acclaim," she concluded.)

Dallaire was a prominent presence at Harvard in 2005, where he completed an academic year as a fellow at the Carr Center before being named a Canadian senator. He always made clear how Rwanda had changed him: "I'm not an academic but a soldier; I hope to light a fire of activism among students." A Roman Catholic, Dallaire criticized the church for not doing enough in Rwanda to lower tensions in the days before the genocide there began. He did not have to mention that Rwandan clergy were complicit in the genocide—that was common knowledge. But he also defended the United Nations, saying it was being turned into a scapegoat for the lack of concern about Darfur. "You can't use the UN some days and then, some days not," he said.

At numerous public forums and informal gatherings, Dallaire spoke about some of the themes Ignatieff and Power addressed, acknowledging the difficulties facing policy-makers: "Once you open fire, you become a third force in the war," he said at one forum. Dallaire was disappointed that the use of the term genocide "had not called us to action" over Darfur, but he agreed with others at Harvard that the debate about the term had probably taken up too much time without stopping the violence. However, the label still had "judicial power" and could be used after the fact, as the subsequent ICC action against al-Bashir proved. Dallaire also spoke openly—sometimes uncomfortably—about his experiences, saying at one public forum, "There is no solace to even consider the idea that I did the best I could." He added: "We failed—but I don't go there. My psychiatrists say: don't go there, so I don't." Yet even while struggling with his own pain, Dallaire was able to view his experiences in a wider context. "I think one day this will stop," he said about war and genocide. "This may take a few centuries. One day we will stop conflict... people want peace and don't want these frictions."

I met Dallaire before he returned to Canada. We chatted on a lawn near Harvard Law School. Dallaire is a solidly built yet soft-spoken, quiet, shy man. I asked him how he felt about being hailed as a hero. Dallaire answered that he had never warmed to the term because of what he called "the failure of the mission." Despite the help of medication and therapy, there were moments when "[I] fall victim to a scene or a memory.... It's a horror show and the boxes open up." He promised himself and others that he would "never let the Rwanda genocide die." Writing a memoir about his time in Rwanda had not been a positive experience: "It was a second descent into hell. I had to relive it."

As we spoke, the Harvard premiere of a documentary about the general was under way. Dallaire said that being the subject of films and the demands made of him as a public speaker were wearying, but he also felt it was his duty—both to the memory of those who died in Rwanda and for those now dying in Darfur. He said he had to honor his commitment to bearing witness. It was clear how great a toll the experience of Rwanda had taken on Dallaire. At night, he could not sleep without a light on.

I asked him about the Roman Catholic Church's complicity in the Rwandan genocide, and he said that the knowledge of that complicity had "humanized my religious belief." By that he meant that the evil and good were now tangible realities. He recalled giving a lecture at Boston College and speaking about God as the "reality of things that are serene, the sensibility of humanity." He believes that human beings seek that serenity and peace. "Anything that attacks it is evil, is the devil." (In his memoir of Rwanda, Dallaire declared that he "shook hands with the devil." In knowing the devil exists, Dallaire said, he also believes "there is a God.")

Dallaire seemed more eager to talk about "serenity" than about evil. "I think there's a momentum with humanity that's evolutionary... the sense of humanity that is really becoming one, beyond borders and ethnicity. Some of that feeling comes from the astronauts in space who saw no borders." He paused. "That's why human rights are so important. If a child in a displaced camp in a terrible situation is able to laugh at something funny and my child, with all the advantages (of being a Canadian), can laugh at the same thing—well, they're the same. It's what surrounds them that makes the difference."

It was a chilly New England afternoon when we spoke, and getting colder—the general wanted to head back indoors. I asked him if he was disappointed about the lack of leadership on Darfur. He groaned. "Oh, if we had statesmen, what we could do." Pointing to Dallaire, I said, "Maybe we do." He laughed and shrugged. "I'm just a rank amateur."

❖   ❖   ❖

I would not call the young Western official I met in 2004 for an informal background briefing on Sudan a rank amateur—he was cordial and appeared to have discussed these things with others as a matter of routine. He told me that the security situation in Darfur "was very fluid," prone to change, and highly unstable. But as I reread my notes from our meeting, I sensed underlying frustration and urgency about what he himself had seen and what the United States and other countries were doing (or not doing) about Darfur. Describing the situation in the camps as "volatile and prime to explode," he stated, "There's a traumatized population in large camps, and people are angry. What people have lost and what they had before is considerable. They realize that they're going to be living a life of squalor." He described Sudan as a police state ruled by wily, adroit, and morally unimaginative men who are always two steps ahead of other governments, the United Nations, and humanitarian groups. "They have no vision beyond staying in power." He described working with the government as surreal. "They'll say there's no war. It's a systematic denial of what's going on. It's incredible; a total whitewash. There is evidence of mass graves, high mortality rates, and they say five thousand people are dead." (They later upped the number to nine thousand.) Yet the situation had a lurching, out-of-control quality to it. "It's very near anarchy; they don't have control over the militias."

❖   ❖   ❖

Losing Steam or Making Quiet Inroads?

The question about political leadership (or the lack of it) was still alive three years later when I asked John Prendergast if he thought the Darfur activist community was losing steam. After all, Darfur activism had been going on for roughly five years. While actions like the ICC's were encouraging, it seemed as if the larger problems were still not solved.

Prendergast acknowledged that "some people were frustrated by the situation," and it was "a real challenge to keep these issues fresh. These are vexing foreign policy questions." Still, he felt the movement was growing, slowly and steadily pressing on the Darfur issue and building a permanent movement to stop and prevent future genocides. He described the movement as "a cross-cutting panoply of actors, including student, faith, and ethnic communities." He also felt that the movement had made quiet inroads: while Darfur was not a prominent campaign issue in 2008, both Barack Obama and John McCain acknowledged it. The Obama and McCain families had all divested from companies doing business in Sudan—a small gesture, but appreciated. Prendergast continued, "I'm relatively optimistic about the nature of the movement, particularly as we're about to change presidents." He noted his and other activists' weariness with the "theatrics and rhetoric" of the Bush administration. "But," he said, "we're not yet passed the finish line."

Just down the street from Prendergast's office in Washington, Mark Hanis, the founder and director of the Genocide Intervention Network, made a similar point: "Stopping genocide is like building a bridge: who cares if you have three-quarters of a bridge? You have to get to the other side. We've had successes, but we're not there yet." His colleague, Chad Hazlett, the Network's field officer and advocacy associate, painted a slightly more optimistic picture, saying, "What happened with the ICC would not have happened had there not been a great deal of noise from U.S. citizens." Hanis and Hazlett are used to finishing each other's sentences, and Hanis added to the list of successes: "A government declared a genocide while it was going on; the response to the Darfur crisis was unprecedented—elementary school kids raised money from bake sales; senior citizens asked presidential candidates at campaign forums what they would do about Darfur." But final success would only come, Hanis continued, "with the cessation of violence and power sharing among the warring factions in Darfur." Of course, there was also the issue of the "full, free return" of those displaced back to their home villages. "Ultimate success is still a long way off," Hanis concluded.

Hanis and a group of Swarthmore College classmates formed the Network in 2004, with the original name of the Genocide Intervention Fund, to "give concerned Americans the opportunity to help protect civilians from genocide." An initial effort to raise $1 million to assist African Union peacekeepers fell short of its goal—the student activists only raised about a quarter of that, and donated the money to humanitarian groups working to protect civilians in Darfur. But the Network has garnered endorsements from not only Samantha Power and General Dallaire but also from two prominent figures who have strongly disagreed, in public and in print, over the nature of the Darfur conflict and its solution—John Prendergast and Alex de Waal.

In an oft-quoted online forum that appeared on *Newsweek*'s website in November 2007, de Waal said that activist groups such as Save Darfur—a coalition of 180 religious, advocacy, and humanitarian organizations, most based in the United States—were actually hindering the peace process because they were not looking at the totality of all of Sudan, placing the fragile North-South peace treaty in jeopardy. He added that "the simplicity of their message is getting in the way of a response." He also pointedly asked, "Has the stress on genocide—which has continued even after the end of large-scale hostilities in early 2005—misrepresented the situation? Has this meant that we have missed more appropriate actions? Does putting Darfur into the same category as the Holocaust and Rwanda mean that we are obliged to do the same for a whole array of ethnic wars and counterinsurgencies across the world?"

Prendergast, disagreed, saying, "These kinds of atrocities have common roots and have common solutions." He chided de Waal for what he called a "bizarrely misplaced" criticism of activists, saying, "It is the policymakers in Washington, Brussels, London, and Beijing who have been primarily responsible for the failure to confront the crime of genocide and the inability to craft relevant solutions to the complicated crisis in Darfur. Activists seek to raise the alarm bell and to shape the policy priorities of their government." (Others in the humanitarian-advocacy community besides de Waal criticized Save Darfur but from a similar position as the humanitarians working on the ground in Darfur – that an overly robust advocacy position could impede efforts to assist those in the camps. The criticism came amid a time of rapid growth and flux for Save Darfur; a 2007 shakeup resulted in the departure of the coalition's then-executive director.)

Amid the various, and heartfelt, disagreements about how best to respond to Darfur, it is hard not to be impressed with Hanis's and Hazlett's enthusiasm and the fact that the young activists—Hanis is twenty-six and Hazlett is twenty-eight—have success-fully navigated the transition from undergraduate activism to a sustained effort that has garnered notice. Of course, their hard work has taken a toll: when I met them, late in the afternoon, they were worn-out after a long day of meetings, with more to come. Hanis seemed the more fatigued of the two and said he had been up until 3 a.m. that morning working. Still, their energy rebounded as Hazlett showed me a PowerPoint presentation about the current situation in Darfur—the presentation was energizing though the news it contained was not. By most accounts, it had become harder to define the situation because Darfur seemed to be collapsing into a mass of inchoate violence, with several different factions fighting each other. Hazlett admitted there was an element of that. But from the data he and others collected from "open sources"—the United Nations, local reporting—he concluded there was still a considerable number of civilians dying in Darfur. "True, overall, indirect violence has been more potent than direct violence," Hazlett said. In other words, more people in Darfur have died from malnutrition and other causes than were actually killed by the *Janjaweed* and military units. Such causes still fit the definition of the 1948 Convention on the Prevention and Punishment of Genocide. But at least through the first half of 2008, attacks by the *Janjaweed* continued, meaning that deaths were not just occurring because civilians were caught in the crossfire. According to Hazlett's data, about one hundred and fifty people were killed in February 2008 alone. "We act like aerial bombardments aren't happening, but they are," he said, in a reference to the fact that *Janjaweed* and military attacks of villages are often accompanied by aerial attacks. While the violence is not anywhere near the level it was in 2004, he concluded, the data appear to point to a continuation of "one-sided attacks." Yes, there are other parties involved, and the long-term solution to Darfur will require "a political settlement that addresses grievances" on all sides, he stressed. But the data suggest that "the core strategy of the government of Sudan remains destroying the Fur, Masalit, and Zaghawa people of Darfur, and not just rebel movements like the JEM."

Hanis said the careful accumulation and distribution of data is part of the stated mission of the network to provide the tools necessary to empower individuals and groups "to stand against genocide" and to help build "the political will necessary for the international community to recognize its responsibility to protect the victims of genocide and mass atrocities." As part of its effort, Hanis wants accessible information and tools to reach political leaders to be as "entertaining" as possible. I asked what he meant by "entertaining." He picked up a phone and dialed "1-800-GENOCIDE." I told Hanis such a number risked parody, but he did not take my bait. He turned on the speakerphone and asked me for my zip code. Punching in the number we were routed to the offices of one of my U.S. senators. "It's something that's both entertaining and effective," Hanis said. "Sixteen thousand calls in two years. I'm proud of this."

I asked Hanis and Hazlett if they felt their movement can continue over the long-term. Hanis emphasized that his group is doing two things simultaneously: focusing on Darfur while trying to build what he called a permanent antigenocide constituency, which is likely to take time. In fact, while Darfur remains a focus of its current work, the Genocide Intervention Network has other areas of concern: Burma, and some of Sudan's neighbors, including Chad, the Central African Republic, and the Democratic Republic of Congo. "Darfur isn't the first genocide, and it won't be the last," Hanis lamented.

Activists and journalists alike are fascinated by Hanis's family background. I asked Hanis about growing up in Ecuador as the descendent of Holocaust survivors, including a grandmother who lives in Scotland. Hanis said she is proud of his work but also a tad skeptical. "She sees a lot of evil in the world and wonders if (my activism) is stopping it or mitigating it." Hanis attended Ecuador's sole synagogue, where all the members were either Holocaust survivors or their descendents. The mantra "never again" was simply part of the worldview he inherited. "Was it nature or nurture? I don't know. But I became an antigenocide activist."

As a student at Swarthmore, Hanis read Samantha Power's *A Problem from Hell*. Hanis and Power have since shared platforms. "She laid it out," he said of Power's argument that throughout modern U.S. history, there has not been a domestic constituency to pressure the government to act on genocide. "And how do you do it?" Hanis asked. "Domestic political will. You need to create the NRA (National Rifle Association) of human rights. You need a domestic political constituency to stop genocide."

◆　　　　◆　　　　◆

One of those likely constituents is Tim Nonn, a coordinator of the "Gathering of Tents," a grassroots effort that in November 2008 erected hundreds of tents on the National Mall in Washington, D.C., to focus attention on Darfur. Groups from three hundred and thirty cities in forty-five states participated in the project, part of a year-long "Tents for Hope" campaign. The "Gathering of Tents" culminated in shipping the tents to Darfur for humanitarian efforts.

Nonn, a veteran peace and justice activist who lives in Petaluma, California, acknowledges the work he and others are involved in is difficult. "When I was younger, and working with Central American refugees, I thought that God wanted me to change the world by working for peace and justice," he said. "That led to burnout because the harder I worked, the worse things got in Central America. It is the same with Darfur. It seems like the harder we work, the worse things get."

What sustains him? First, "many Darfur activists sustain themselves through connections with one another. We give each other hope. Second, the Darfuris who survive unimaginable hardship, suffering, and terror help to keep us going. We cannot desert them." Nonn acknowledges there are difficulties within the Darfur activist movement—troubles that exist in any broad-based effort. Among them: "Organizational territorialism and a disconnect between local communities and national organizations," he said. Nonn believes that activists always have to keep in mind that "compassion emerges in communities, not organizations."

Despite the attendant frustrations and problems, Nonn sees a larger force at play— particularly as so many Darfur activists are doing this work as an expression of their religious faith. "Governments are always going to use violence to achieve their ends. Genocide is an extreme example of such power. The challenge is to perceive the sacredness of creation and one another. Perceiving the sacred bond that connects all of us and all of life builds us up," he said. "That's why I have always felt that compassion is the moral force of the Darfur movement. It's not only a feeling. Compassion reveals the truth of our oneness as humankind. I am absolutely certain that God is doing a great work in Darfur and in the Darfur movement."

CHAPTER

4

Calling the Faithful

We are caught in H. Richard Niebuhr's web of creation. As such we are responsible for each other and ourselves. . . . We have to give an accounting of ourselves and our actions and inactions.

—Emilie Townes, *Womanist Ethics and the Cultural Production of Evil* (2006)

Tim Nonn is not alone in believing there is a deeper significance to the U.S. Darfur movement. He shouldn't be. The lion's share of Darfur activism has been performed by faith-based organizations forming unusual alliances. Christian, Jewish, and Muslim groups that do not agree on a host of issues have come together on Darfur and the drive to stop genocide. Whether this unusual coalition can be sustained is anyone's guess. But activists like Cory Smith believe that there has long been a need for planting "God Roots" within what has been a predominately secular human rights community.

"It's as clear as night and day: if you want to engage people in this country on human rights, you have to engage people of faith," Smith, the ENOUGH Project's faith outreach advisor, said in his Washington office. Given what he called the "moral imperative" within the U.S. Jewish community to respond to genocide, he praised what he called "amazing work by Jewish groups." They're 2 percent of the population, but it feels like they've done 80 percent of the work." However, Smith believes that a sustained movement concerned with genocide and human rights must ultimately engage what is still the religious majority in the United States: U.S. Christians, in all of their theological, social, racial, and political diversity. "Secular human rights groups want the churches involved, but only at the eleventh hour. It's never a fair or equal partnership. But look at the numbers. If the Christian churches move on this, it's an enormous constituency.

Add up the membership of the top eight to ten Christian denominations and if even a small number of them become involved—10 million—that's a substantial group. That's what you need. All Congress responds to is numbers."

But the potential is not just in numbers. Smith believes "the churched" bring something valuable to activist work facing "intractable problems"— endurance. "When you face something intractable, faith can overcome the cynicism or fatigue that sets in after five years and the perception that the problem is just too overwhelming." Was this possible given the erosion of trust in religious institutions, given recent scandals? "Sure, there's been cynicism about these scandals. But the church is still an institution that is respected and part of people's lives. It's there for the long term."

Smith, thirty-six, grew up as a Baptist "military brat." Now a United Methodist, he believes the coalition of secular and religious groups that sustained the civil rights movement of the 1950s and 1960s was later eclipsed for a host of reasons, including the ascendancy of conservative evangelicalism. Often lost in the shuffle were the established, mainline Protestant churches that had been involved in the civil rights movement but whose membership and media visibility declined as the evangelicals began their rise. Evangelicals have not embraced the more liberal-leaning human rights constituency, though as Smith pointed out, they have championed a number of human rights causes, including the massive violation of human rights in southern Sudan. In turn, secular human right groups have tended to have "an allergic reaction" to churches given their equating "church" with theological and political conservatism. In secular circles, the prominent figures of Jimmy Swaggert and the late Jerry Falwell proved unpalatable. "It was a turnoff for people," Smith said, adding that even now, human rights blogs tend to be "very hostile to a lot of faith and church movements." He added: "When you're a Christian, you're seen as only one stripe."

Smith believes some of these divisions between liberals and conservatives may be less important than they once were: evangelicals in their teens and twenties, he said, are growing weary of the partisanship that has marked evangelical activism in the last generation, not to mention identification with the Republican Party. Instead, they are embracing issues like combating poverty and genocide, issues that have a moral stripe but can reach across theological and denominational lines. "Younger evangelicals are saying: 'I care about life; I care about poverty; I care about genocide.'"

Was it easier to care about Darfur because the violence was committed by Muslims against Muslims—in other words, it was "someone else's violence," making it easier to be nonsectarian? "Possibly," Smith replied, "but it's been a principled response. If there had been no reaction on Darfur by Christians after southern Sudan, you could be cynical," he said. "But the Christian community has been very engaged. Muslim groups have been involved: they have not been as visible, but what percentage of Americans are Muslim? It's small. Of course, for the Jewish community, there's been a moral imperative."

He mentioned the role of a respected conservative evangelical who has been prominent on Darfur: Richard Cizik, the one-time vice president of governmental affairs for the National Association of Evangelicals. Cizik has earned the respect of more liberal religious leaders for being a straight shooter. His NAE business card read: "Cooperation Without Compromise." But within some evangelical circles, Cizik is unpopular for speaking his mind and forging alliances with liberal Christians and non-Christians if the issue is right, perhaps most famously on environmental concerns. (Cizik resigned his NAE post in late 2008 after saying he supported same-sex civil unions.) Darfur is another issue where Cizik has worked in coalition with non-evangelicals. Smith said of Cizik: "He's a principled man. I disagree with him on some social issues, but on Darfur, he's been wonderful to work with."

Ruth Messinger, the head of American Jewish World Service, a New York–based humanitarian group, recalled a difficult meeting on Darfur between religious leaders and a prominent State Department official. "Dick Cizik played the Secretary for all he was worth." Bob Edgar, an ordained United Methodist minister and the former general secretary of the National Council of Churches, agreed: "Dick Cizik is a good man, and a smart man."

He is. In between appointments during a July visit to New York City, Cizik spoke passionately and with some understandable frustration about Darfur. Seated in a leather chair in a Manhattan hotel lobby, he practically leaped when he declared Darfur "was and *is* genocide."

"We've always said, 'never again.' But it's in our own face, right now. Are we going to stand by and do nothing? Or push whatever levels we have to in order for the United States to act?" Pausing for effect, he continued, "Sigh. Here we are, four years later. How do we respond to a crisis that has led to death, and, aside from genocide, the destruction of 1 million people?" He later said: "Are we supposed to pretend this is not happening? This is what happened in the 1930s (in Nazi Germany). 'Not on our watch'—that's what Bush said. But it *has* happened on our watch."

Darfur has become a personal cause for Cizik partly because he believes strongly that the most salient dimensions of the crisis are environmental—that drought has forced nomads to alter their migration patterns and has set them against established farming communities. "Darfur represents the future of the twenty-first century, if we're not careful," Cizik warned. "These conflicts are rooted in fights over natural resources. You can see the conflicts not only in Darfur but in Niger and other countries. The idea you can ignore issues like climate change is foolish. We have to see our way through this or else we'll see it all over again elsewhere."

Cizik said this just days after the ICC's warrant for President al-Bashir's arrest was issued—an action Cizik warmly welcomed. But overall, Darfur had not garnered much media attention in the previous six months or made it to the top of discussions in the U.S. presidential campaign, he noted. Cizik was frustrated on both counts, particularly with the media's apparent lack of care or curiosity about Darfur. "One has to ask what certain media representatives are doing right now," Cizik complained.

But these frustrations paled in comparison to his reaction—by turns, annoyed, frustrated, and angered—to the Bush administration's response to Darfur. The National Association of Evangelicals—whose members, after all, represented one of President Bush's "base" constituencies—had sent letters about Darfur to the president and asked to meet with him. But they had not received a response.

The August 2004 letter to Bush was hardly the stuff of saber rattling, though it was tough. The letter said it was "irresponsible to expect that the Government of Sudan, which has backed the *Janjaweed* militia, to restore peace in the Darfur. Since Khartoum cannot be counted on to provide security, others must lead the way." The letter also urged Bush to increase humanitarian assistance; explore "*all* available intervention options" to stop the killing, including sending troops to Darfur or expanding the African Union protection force. It also asked the United States to seek the removal of Sudan from membership on the UN Human Rights Commission. "Sudan's genocidal policies make its continued participation on that body a travesty," the letter said.

I asked Cizik, who voted for Bush twice, why he thought there had been no response from the Bush administration to the letter and why the Bush administration's approach to Darfur had disappointed so many activists and religious leaders like himself. "I think President Bush has taken the right steps to acknowledge what it is, which is genocide. But he hasn't done much else. He and other policymakers are distracted by Iraq." Cizik was only warming up. "We fought an unnecessary war," for which Darfur was suffering the consequences, he said. Cizik returned again to the meeting the NAE requested but never got: "It bespeaks a certain arrogance in my mind," he complained. "The president doesn't listen, and it's pretty obvious he doesn't care."

Another reason Darfur has been a particular point of disappointment for U.S. evangelicals has been the stark contrast to U.S. policy on southern Sudan—something of a success for the Bush administration and for the evangelical community, whose grassroots pressure kept the issue alive during both the Clinton and Bush presidencies. Bush's high-profile appointment of former Senator John Danforth, an Episcopal priest, as a special envoy was symbolic, many believed, of how seriously Bush took the issue and had listened to his influential evangelical Christian base. Why Bush had not heard them on Darfur was cause for speculation. One U.S. journalist theorized: "Unfortunately, black African Muslim farmers in Darfur didn't have the same Washington lobby as the evangelicals."

Cizik acknowledged that Darfur, at least at first, posed a challenge for U.S. evangelicals. Some outside and some inside the evangelical movement asked, "You cared about the church in southern Sudan, but do you care about the black Muslims of Darfur?" There were also concerns "that activism about Darfur could jeopardize the progress made on southern Sudan." Some said move cautiously. In the end, Cizik and others came to the conclusion that "we didn't have any option. You don't sit on your hands when the gross extermination of a people is taking place. Do you have an option otherwise? No.

We clearly said that when Christians and non-Christians alike are victims, we have to exhibit concern irrespective of religions."

Such commitment, Cizik said, stems from what he called the religious community's common identity. "Collectively, we *do* believe we are our brother's keeper," he said. "It can't only be justice in theory." For Christians steeped in a world of biblical injunctions, acting means taking the idea of responsibility personally. "From beginning to end, from Genesis to the book of Revelation, the Bible affirms the importance of a single life. The Scriptures affirm the sanctity of one human life regardless of race, religion, or ethnic origin." He paused. "Let me show you something." Cizik pulled from his wallet a quote from Carl F. H. Henry, a well-known twentieth-century evangelical leader who issued a call to the "uneasy conscience of the modern fundamentalist." It reads: "The cries of suffering humanity today are many. No Evangelicalism which ignores the totality of man's condition dares respond in the name of Christianity."

Cizik also told me about another well-known evangelical leader, the Philadelphia clergyman Donald Gray Barnhouse, who quietly raised money and did what he could to help Jews leave Europe in the 1930s. That was one case of an otherwise disappointing record. In a 1981 study on the response of American Protestant churches to the rise of Nazism, historian William Nawyn concluded: "Protestant response was substantial in some quarters, virtually absent or severely attenuated in others. Apathy was widespread, yet some were deeply committed."

Was that also the case in Darfur? "Should we have done more? Maybe so. But we're still fighting this," Cizik said. "It's a collective failure: the world community, the U.S. government, our own public leaders, including the president." He hailed the fact that the religious community in the United States—divided over "hot-button" issues that include abortion, gay rights, and the Israeli and Palestinian conflict—"came together in a remarkable way."

"Have we stopped what happened? No. Did we do what we could? Yes. But you can't make leaders do what they don't want to do."

The Courageous Remnants That Change the World

Speaking to Ruth Messinger and Bob Edgar in the same week was a reminder that Jews and Christians, deeply committed to the issue of Darfur, share a prophetic tradition in which empathy is biblically rooted and mandated, as in the injunction in Exodus 23:9 that "you shall not oppress a resident alien; you know the heart of an alien, for you were aliens in the land of Egypt." Edgar and Messinger, both in their sixties, are of a generation that came of age in an era of pronounced activism—a time when religious figures like theologian Abraham Joshua Heschel formed alliances with Martin Luther King Jr. and others. Heschel explained his activism by saying that the task of humanity "is to be a voice for the plundered poor," and that "there is no limit to the concern one must feel for (the) suffering of human beings."

A DISPLACED WOMAN in Labado weeps as she tells the story of how the Janjaweed attacked her village. More than 2.5 million Darfur residents have been displaced since 2003 by a coalition of government forces and Arab militias.

THE CONFLICT in Darfur has been triggered by those who want to exploit cultural differences for political purposes, differences that aren't always readily apparent. These two boys have so much in common, yet one (left) is culturally African and lives in a displacement camp in Kubum, while the other (right) is culturally Arab and lives in the village of Dondona.

THE ISLAMIC GOVERNMENT in Khartoum fought a long and bloody civil war against mostly Christian rebels in the south of the country, but the conflict in Darfur pits Muslims against Muslims. In the sweltering camps for the internally displaced, faith provides something steady to cling to. Farmah Adam Ibrahim and Sit-Eldoma Atiya pray in a displaced camp near Bilel.

TWO PEOPLES with two different understandings of the land's vocation have co-existed for centuries in Darfur, their relationship at times symbiotic, at other times violent. Although stark differentiation isn't possible, and intermarriage and shifting land use has altered the pattern in recent years, one group is culturally Arab, mostly nomads and herders *(left)*, while the other is culturally African, mostly farmers, like Khadilla Abdulah Ibrahim and her daughter Hawaia *(below)*, who plow a small plot on the edge of the displaced camp where they live near Bilel. When African-supported rebel groups took up arms against Sudan's central government in 2003, Khartoum couldn't respond with its army, which had a large number of recruits from Darfur's African villages, so instead it pushed militias from the Arab communities to launch a massive counterinsurgency campaign which has killed as many as 400,000 people.

A ONCE LIFE-FILLED village near Zalingei, one of hundreds of farming villages that has been attacked and burned during a counterinsurgency campaign in Darfur, forcing survivors to flee to displacement camps in Darfur or refugee camps across the border in Chad.

THE REMAINS of a clinic *(above)* and a house *(left)* in the village of Labado, which according to an African Union report was bombed by Sudanese government planes in 2004. | THE FOUNDATION WALLS *(below)* of a family's hut are all that remain in the burned-out village of Um Seifa, one of hundreds of African farm villages destroyed in Darfur.

IN 2004 the United Nations responded to the crisis in Darfur by dispatching a contingent of troops from the African Union, including these Nigerian soldiers on patrol in Labado in 2005. Yet the AU troops suffered from a weak mandate and chronic funding problems. They were eventually replaced by a hybrid UN-AU force beginning in late 2007, but the new "peacekeepers" suffered from many of the same limitations, as well as a more complicated political landscape which offered no peace to keep. | HUMANITARIAN AGENCIES have suffered from the violence of the war, with staff kidnappings and vehicle hijackings occurring at an increasing rate. This truck, carrying food to the village of Labado, was attacked and burned in 2005. | TIME IS SLOWLY dissolving the remains of simple homes in Bela, an African village destroyed in a 2003 militia attack that killed 37 people and drove the terrorized survivors into miserable camps for the displaced.

A CAMP FOR INTERNALLY displaced families outside Zalingei. Many of these camps have tens of thousands of residents who can't leave for fear of being assaulted or raped outside the camp. And massive war-provoked displacement in Darfur has accelerated urbanization. At the turn of the century, Darfur was less than 18 percent urbanized. Today it's 65 percent urbanized, and even if

the conflict were to end tomorrow, many people would be reluctant to return to their old village life. Experts suggest that even in the best of circumstances, half of Darfur's population will continue living in cities, a fact that bodes ill for resource allocation—something that has long been at the center of reoccurring conflict throughout the desert region.

THE VIOLENCE IN DARFUR has been mirrored inside Chad, where similar ethnic tensions exist on both sides of the arbitrarily drawn international border. Food from Japan and the United States, administered by an ecumenical agency in coordination with the World Food Program of the United Nations, is unloaded at the Habile camp for Chadian families displaced by that violence, on the edge of the village of Koukou Angarana. *(right)* | AIDING THE DISPLACED and refugees from Darfur is the world's largest humanitarian operation. Here food awaits distribution to families living in a displaced camp outside the town of Garsila. *(below)*

A WOMAN DIVIDES up rations of food distributed by the World Food Program and an ecumenical aid organization in the Aradib Camp for internally displaced persons outside the village of Goz Amer, Chad *(above)*. Some 28,000 people live in precarious conditions in this camp. In a conflict that mirrors the Darfur violence, more than 180,000 residents of eastern Chad have been displaced by violence spilling over from neighboring Darfur, inter-ethnic conflict, and fighting between rebels and the Chadian government. They often live alongside a quarter million Darfur refugees in Chad. | RESIDENTS OF A CAMP for displaced families outside Garsila line up for water, a critical commodity in the desert. *(below)*

RECENTLY DISPLACED by violence, a newly arrived resident of a camp near Garsila constructs a shelter for his family *(above)*. | A GIRL IN FRONT of her family's home in the Dereig camp for displaced people *(bottom)*.

FRESHLY CHASED OUT of their home villages by the Janjaweed, people construct shelters in the Hassa Hissa camp outside Zalingei.

NEWLY ARRIVED RESIDENTS build their house in the Habile Camp for internally displaced Chadians outside the village of Koukou Angarana. The conflict in eastern Chad is intimately related to the conflict in Darfur *(right)*.

A GIRL CARRIES water in the Habile Camp for internally displaced Chadians, located just outside the village of Koukou Angarana. Water is often a scarce commodity in the desert, and many of the displaced living in organized camps in Darfur and Chad have clean and safe water provided by the international community's largest humanitarian operation. That particularly eases the burden on women and girls, who traditionally fetch water, a task that in their villages of origin may have taken several hours per day.

WOMEN AND GIRLS crowd around a water distribution point *(above)*, constructed by an ecumenical relief alliance, in the Hamidiya camp for displaced families near Zalingei. Water is strictly rationed, and usually only available certain periods of each day. | WOMEN CARRY WATER home in the Hassa Hissa Camp for internally displaced persons *(below)*, outside Zalingei.

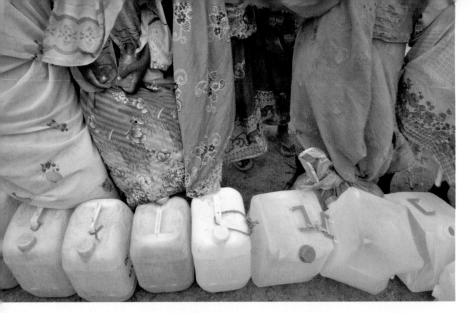

WOMEN WHO RETURNED to their bombed-out village of Labado after an AU mission moved in line up for water at a well dug by an ecumenical relief network.

GIRLS SCOOPING WATER from a hole they dug in the sand of a wadi in Dondona, an Arab village in South Darfur. The community has received families displaced by fighting between other Arab communities as the pro-government alliance of Arab villages began to dissolve in 2007.

WAITING FOR WATER to be turned on in the Hassa Hissa camp near Zalingei.

A WOMAN GETS WATER at a community tap in
the Hassa Hissa camp for displaced families.

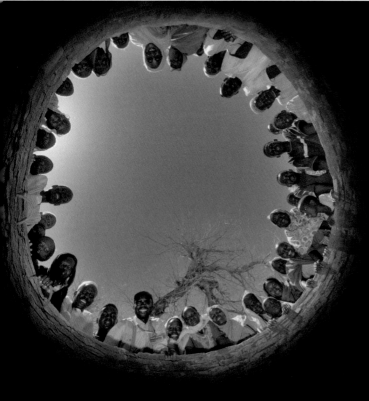

CONFLICTS OVER WATER have plagued Darfur for centuries, as herders and farmers struggled for control of the vital resource. As the current political crisis exploded in 2003, hundreds of thousands of displaced farmers began to establish camps at the edge of Arab villages, "host communities" in relief agency lingo, and tensions over water threatened to push the already troubled relationship into open violence. Some relief agencies, which came in to help the displaced, also provided new wells and water systems for the Arab communities as a way of working toward reconciliation. That was the case here, in Um Labassa, where an ecumenical relief network provided several wells for the host community, including this one *(above)*. | IT TAKES A VILLAGE to dig a well. Residents of the Khamsadegaig camp for internally displaced families look down a well they constructed with assistance from an ecumenical relief group which helped them with a variety of services, including potable water, sanitation, and income generating opportunities. *(left)*

CHILDREN IN THE ARADIB CAMP for internally displaced persons outside the village of Goz Amer, in eastern Chad, taking a bath near a community well. Chad has a quarter million refugees from Darfur as well as at least 180,000 internally displaced people, survivors of the same conflict that has plagued families on the other side of the arbitrary international border in Darfur.

WATER CAN BE A TRIGGER for war, and a way to build peace. Women carry water home in Geles, an Arab village in Darfur where an ecumenical group has provided wells and a variety of other services. While humanitarian operations in Darfur are

focused primarily on responding to the needs of the region's internally displaced people, in some cases it also is helping Arab villages, many of them host communities for the camps, as a contribution toward reconciliation between the two groups.

GIRLS IN CLASS in the Dereig Camp *(above)* for internally displaced persons. In their villages of origin, many Darfur girls did not have access to education, and life in the camps, as hard as it is, has raised the quality of life for many girls and women, a fact which will likely have long-term social impacts in Darfurian society once the displaced can return home and rebuild their villages in peace. The provision of education, health care, and water in the camps also makes the displaced less likely to voluntarily return to their villages unless many of those services are made available there—an issue that has been raised frequently by refugee representatives during off-and-on peace talks. | A SCHOOL in the Dereig Camp *(below)* for internally displaced persons. Many schools have separate classes for boys and girls.

A GIRL ARRIVES at school in the morning in the Dereig Camp for internally displaced persons.

APPARENTLY ENJOYING the luxury of attending school, girls hurry to class *(right)* in the Dereig Camp for internally displaced persons. | CHILDREN PLAY OUTSIDE their school in a camp near Bilel *(below)*.

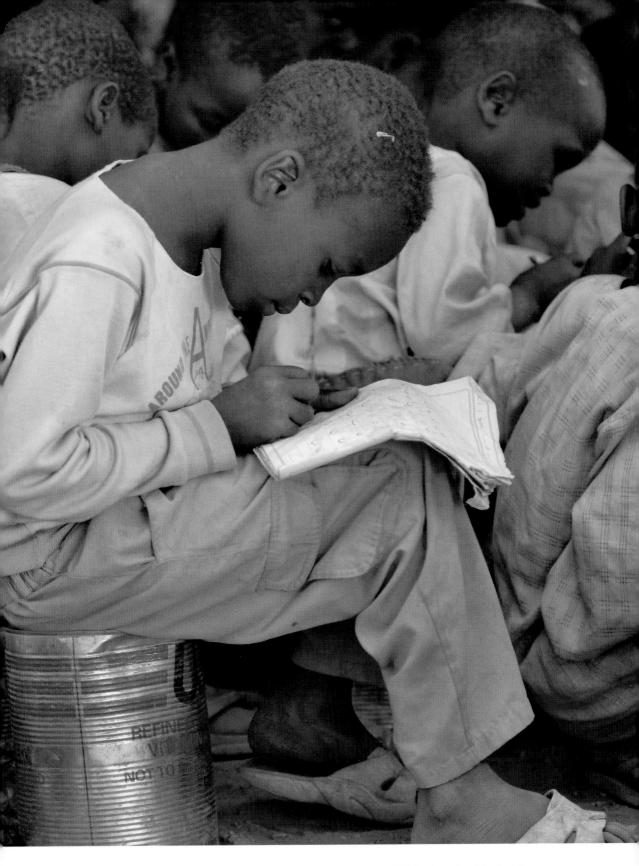

CHILDREN STUDYING in the school in the Hassa Hissa camp for displaced families near Zalingei.

CHILDREN LIVING in the Habile camp for internally displaced persons go to school in the village of Koukou Angarana, Chad *(above)*. More than 80 percent of the students here are displaced children or refugees. | UNDER THE WATCHFUL eye of his teacher, a student shows off his math skills in a school in the Dereig Camp for internally displaced persons *(below)*.

CHILDREN LIVING in the Habile camp for internally displaced persons go to school in the village of Koukou Angarana, Chad *(above).* | CHILDREN PLAY OUTSIDE their school in a camp near Bilel *(below).*

GIRLS PLAY OUTSIDE their school in a camp near Bilel *(above)*. | A BOY IN A DISPLACED camp outside Zalingei practices walking on his hands *(below)*. Life in the camps can grow very tedious for children as they grow older, nurturing resentment and often encouraging young people to support insurgent movements that promise justice.

CHILDREN IN THE KUBUM camp for internally displaced families crossing a wadi at the edge of the camp. During the short rainy season, Darfur turns green and the wadis fill with water.

A DISPLACED GIRL walking through the desert near Labado in search of water.

A DISPLACED BOY in Labado.

A GIRL SKIPS rope *(above)*, part of daily life in the Dereig Camp for internally displaced persons, one of many such settlements for people displaced by the violence in Darfur. Camp residents are usually unable to leave the confines of the Untied Nations-supervised camps because of roving militia bands that often assault, rape, and kill the displaced who attempt to travel outside the relative safety of the camps. | A BOY AT PLAY in a camp for internally displaced people outside Um Labassa *(below)*.

CHILDREN PLAYING in a camp for the displaced outside Zalingei *(above)*. | CHILDREN IN A CAMP for internally displaced people outside Kubum *(below)*. More than 2.25 million people are living in camps like this in the Darfur region, with another quarter million surviving in refugee camps across the border in Chad.

A GIRL IN THE HABILE CAMP for internally displaced Chadians outside the village of Koukou Angarana *(above)*. Some 25,000 people live in this one camp, displaced by the same conflict which has torn apart Darfur. | DARFUR DISCIPLINE: the school director "encourages" students to get into their classroom on time in the Dereig Camp for internally displaced persons.

DAILY LIFE in the Dereig camp *(above)*. | WHEN IT RAINS: a girl in the
Hassa Hissa Camp for internally displaced persons, outside Zalingei *(below)*.

DISPLACED AFRICAN FARM families can farm land only within sight of the displaced camp where they're living, as is the case for this woman who lives in the camp outside Um Labassa. To venture farther into the desert would be to risk assault and rape.

A WOMAN PREPARES the ground beside her hut for planting in the Habile Camp for internally displaced Chadians outside the village of Koukou Angarana.

KHADIDJE GAMAR, a resident of the Habile Camp for internally displaced persons outside the village of Koukou Angarana, Chad, *(above)* participates with her child Matar Hamed in a community garden project sponsored by an ecumenical relief alliance. | A BOY PREPARES the soil next to his family's home for planting in the Dereig Camp for internally displaced persons *(right)*. The land available for planting is very limited, since families can't travel far from the camps for security reasons, and thus international assistance is necessary to keep people from starving.

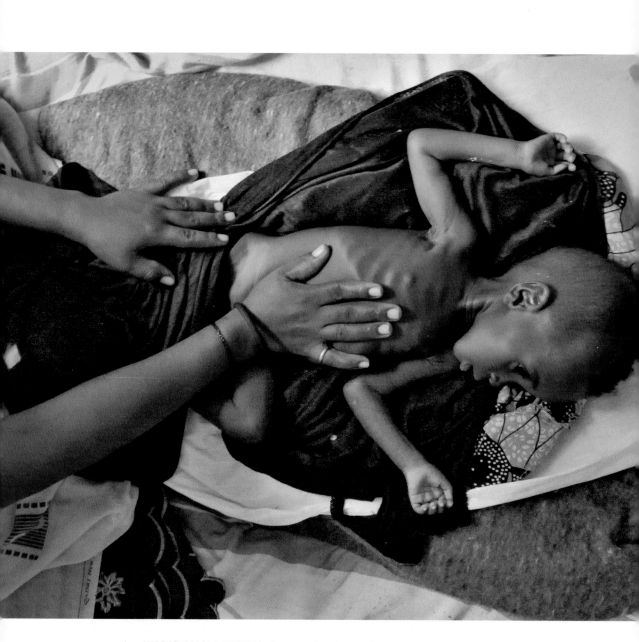

WAR'S SMALL VICTIM: A young boy is comforted by his mother in a feeding center for malnourished children in the Goz Amer refugee camp in eastern Chad. Some 250,000 Darfur refugees live in Chad, alongside more than 180,000 Chadians who've been displaced by a war which ignores international borders–"genocide without borders," according to some.

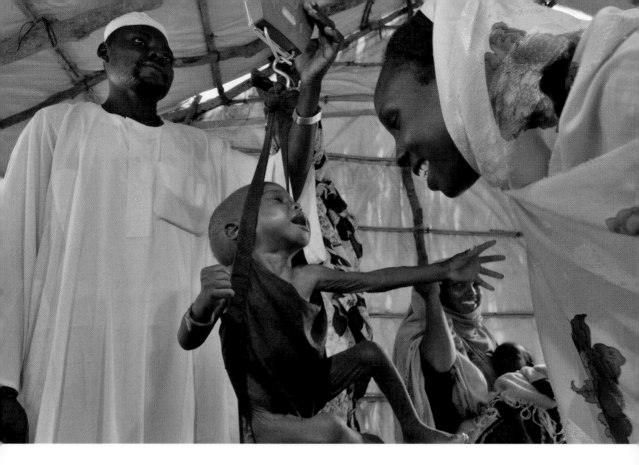

THE HEIGHT AND WEIGHT of displaced children is carefully monitored at a nutrition and health center in the Um Labassa camp. Mothers with at-risk babies are given supplemental food by the ecumenical relief network that sponsors the center.

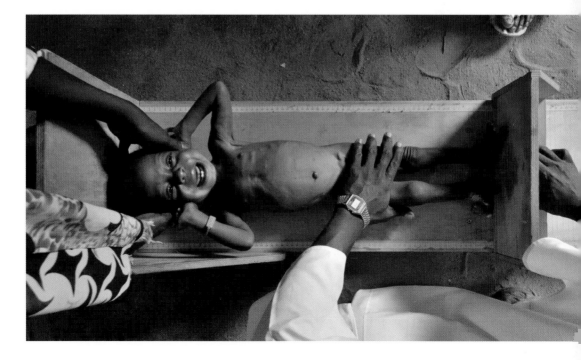

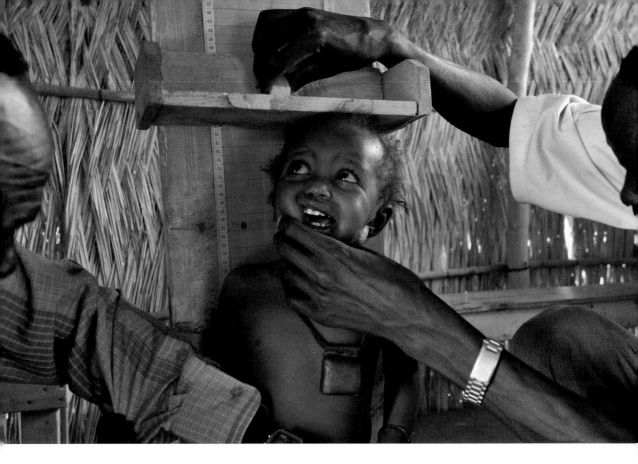

IN THE BILEL CAMP near Nyala *(above)*, an ecumenical relief group sponsors a feeding center where displaced children have their height and weight monitored and where they receive supplementary food. | IN THE ARDABBA CAMP near Garsila *(below)*, an ecumenical relief group provides primary health care, including the services of a physician, to displaced families as well as the local host community.

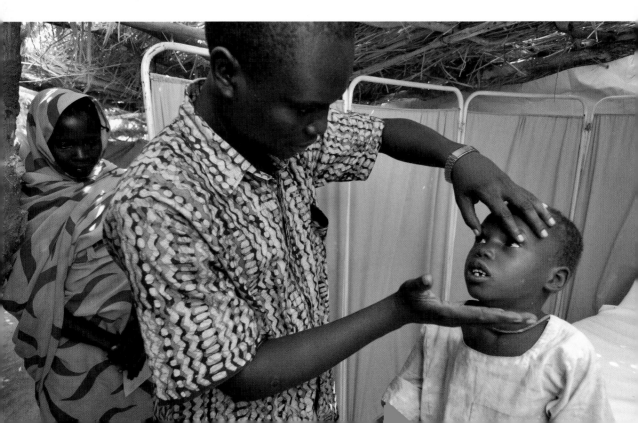

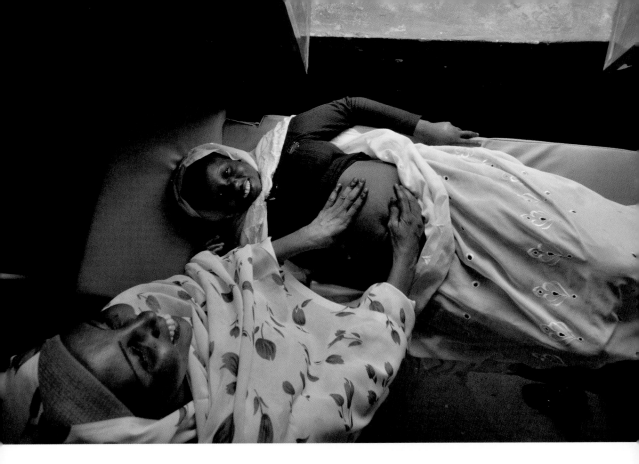

PRENATAL CARE is an important part of the mission of a primary health care and nutrition center in Um Labassa.

A CLINIC RUN by the Catholic Church in Nyala treats displaced persons, including children, for skin diseases—a common problem in the burgeoning camps.

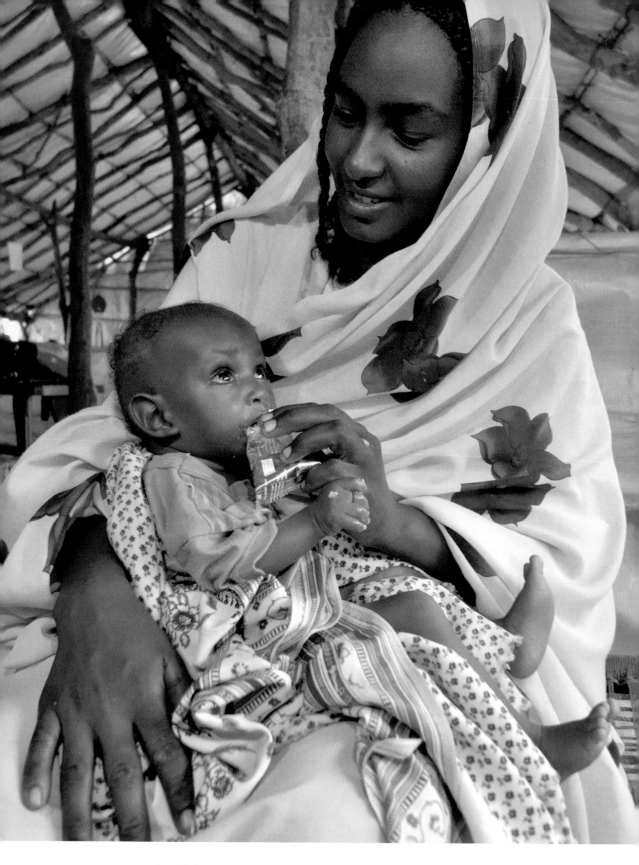

IN A PRIMARY HEALTH care and nutrition center in Um Labassa, a mother gives her malnourished baby "Plumpy'nut," a nutrition supplement developed in the last decade and today used widely in situations of famine and hunger.

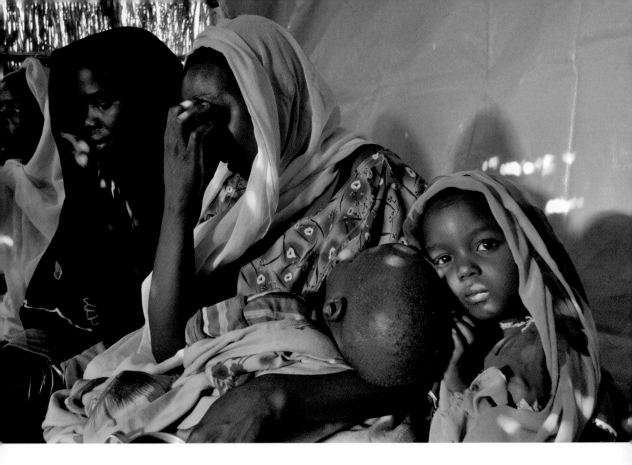

WAITING TO SEE the doctor. In the Ardabba camp near Garsila, an ecumenical relief alliance provides primary health care to displaced families as well as members of the local host community. Yet there is often a wait.

AT A NUTRITION CENTER in Kubum sponsored an ecumenical network, an expectant mother walks home with a supplemental food package that will help her baby get a healthy start on life.

DISPLACED WOMEN carrying pots they have made walk through the streets of Zalingei in order to sell them to local residents.

RELIEF GROUPS WORKING in the camps often try to help camp residents develop small businesses and provide skills training for the day to come when they'll go home—and a bit of dignity in the meantime. Here some boys bake bread in a camp for internally displaced people outside Um Labassa.

A MAN SPINS THREAD *(left)* in a community center in the Jabaleen camp near Garsila, one of many income-generating activities for displaced families. | WOMEN IN A LIVELIHOOD program *(above)* in the Dereig Camp for internally displaced persons. | A MAN BAKES BREAD in the Khamsadegaig displaced camp *(below)*, yet another income-generating activity.

A WOMAN SWEEPS the dirt around her home in the Dereig Camp. Women in the camps bear an inordinate share of daily tasks. In some cases, no men are present; they were killed or are mobilized in rebel groups. In other cases, it's just simple discrimination.

FATNA BATHES and dresses her son Mustafa in a camp for internally displaced persons outside Kubum, where an ecumenical group is providing water, sanitation and other emergency services.

GENDER-BASED CHORES aren't unique to Africans in Darfur. Here a girl irons in her family's hut in Dondona, an Arab village in Darfur that has taken in dozens of other families displaced by fighting between Arab communities over whether they should remain as participants in the government's counterinsurgency strategy.

FATNA EATS WITH her children *(above)* in a camp for internally displaced persons outside Kubum. She prepares a meal inside her hut *(below)*.

A WOMAN'S WORK is never done: grinding grain to cook and eat in the Dereig Camp for internally displaced persons.

OUTSIDE THE KALMA camp *(above)* and a camp near Garsila *(below)*, women return with firewood they've gathered. As camps have grown in size, women–the traditional fetchers of wood and water–have had to travel farther to find wood, exposing themselves even more to being assaulted and raped by roving bands of Janjaweed and others who lurk in wait outside the camps. Such violence against women has increasingly become a systematic tool of war in Darfur and other places in Africa. And it's more: "It's often a method of ethnic humiliation and elimination. Attackers say they are implanting themselves and their tribe in you and in effect ending you as a race," said Jan Egeland, former United Nations Under Secretary General for Humanitarian Affairs.

NURSING HER CHILD, a woman cooks over an "improved stove" in the Goz Amer refugee camp in eastern Chad. Given the life-threatening danger involved in fetching wood, non-governmental organizations have distributed tens of thousands of metal stoves—or trained women to build them out of bricks–that consume less firewood, thus reducing the number of trips outside the camps. Women who have access to income can usually buy charcoal, at least in the larger camps, but the felling of trees to produce the charcoal has contributed to widespread deforestation in a huge radius around the camps.

WOMEN BRING HOME FIREWOOD they have scavenged outside the Kubum camp for displaced families. Women who have been raped while hunting for firewood have often faced a second discrimination; blamed for being sexually assaulted, they and their baby are rejected by their own tribe. An ecumenical relief network has conducted training sessions on rape and the law for hundreds of police officers in Darfur, while at the same time training people in the camps as advocates for women who have been assaulted.

A WOMAN IN LABADO weeps as she tells how government-backed Arab militias attacked her village *(left)*. | HAWA ABDALL NOLA ADAM holds her baby to her *(below)* as she adjusts her garments at the edge of the Hassa Hissa Camp for internally displaced persons, outside Zalingei, where she and her family arrived in 2007 after having resisting displacement for four years.

JOY SURVIVES DISPLACEMENT. In the Abu Jabra camp for the displaced *(above)*, women put the finishing touches on a thatched roof—and celebrate as they do so. | THE HUMAN SPIRIT is resilient. Despite surviving extreme violence and living in a camp, women celebrate the everyday joys of life as they sing and dance in the Kubum camp *(below)*.

NEAR THE EL FERDOUS camp for the displaced, a girl—carrying water back home on her donkey—takes a moment to laugh at a photographer.

A WOMAN'S WORK is on the farm. A displaced woman on her way to work her small field on the edge of the Habile Camp for internally displaced Chadians outside the village of Koukou Angarana. The conflict in Chad is directly linked to the ethnic and political conflict in neighboring Darfur.

AN ARAB MAN, with his camel, listening to news on the radio. Many Arabs in Darfur have grown weary of the alliance with the government, and several Arab militia leaders have broken from the government. One Arab group even joined the anti-government rebel movement.

IN A CAMP for the displaced near Bilel, families have taken refuge from the violence, and are assisted by an ecumenical relief group with a variety of emergency services, including seeds and agricultural tools, schools and pre-schools for their children, and health care. Here, four-year old Mohammed Husain sleeps under a blanket provided by the faith-based humanitarian group. | IT RAINS IN THE DESERT for three months or so. Here a woman runs through the rain in the Khamsadegaig camp.

THIS GIRL AND HER younger sibling live in a displaced camp outside Garsila, where the pot is often empty.

A WOMAN LIVING in the Hassa Hissa camp outside Zalingei.

WOMEN GRIND GRAIN in the Habile Camp for internally displaced persons outside the village of Koukou Angarana, in eastern Chad. The conflict in eastern Chad is part of the same larger conflict in Darfur. | TWO DISPLACED WOMEN sharing a hut in a camp outside Garsila *(below)*.

DISPLACED BOYS peer through a fence around a feeding center for malnourished children in the Bilel camp near Nyala.

A "STREET" in the Goz Amer refugee camp in eastern Chad. More than a quarter million residents of Darfur live in camps in Chad, along with almost 200,000 Chadians who have been internally displaced by related violence.

A MOTHER and her daughter in Geles, an Arab village in Darfur where an ecumenical relief organization has provided wells and a variety of other services. While the world's largest humanitarian operation is focused primarily on responding to the needs of Darfur's internally displaced people, some agencies are also helping Arab villages, many of them host communities, as a contribution toward reconciliation and peace. An ecumenical relief organization has also established local conflict mediation teams involving members from both the African and Arab communities.

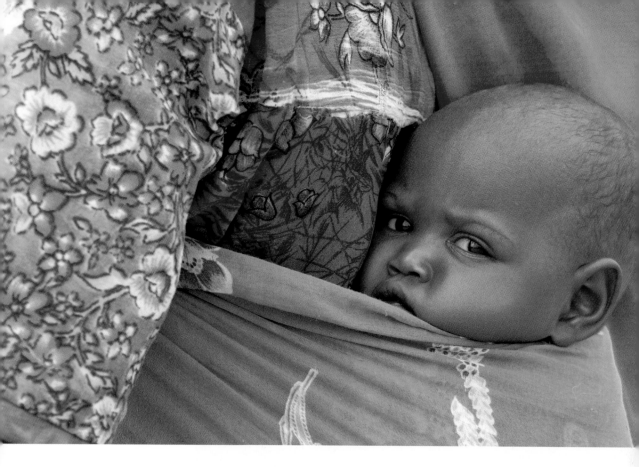

A BABY on its mother's back
in the Bilel camp.

TWO YEAR OLD
Abdulbasid lives in
a camp for internally
displaced persons
outside Kubum.

A WOMAN HEADS to her small field in the Hamadiya camp for internally displaced families.

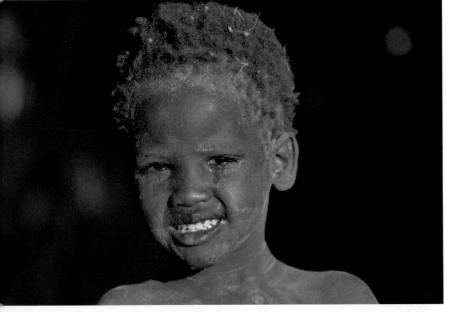

A BOY DISPLACED by an armed attack on his village still suffers from the trauma in a camp for the displaced near Al Daein.

AN ARAB MAN in Dondona, a village in Darfur that has received families displaced by fighting between other Arab communities over the beginning of a breakdown of the Janjaweed alliance in 2007.

GLOBALIZATION HAS NO LIMITS: a girl in
the Jabaleen displaced camp near Garsila.

A DISPLACED WOMAN strings a cot as a United Nations helicopter flies over the Dereig Camp *(left)*. | A GIRL GROWING up in a camp for displaced persons near Kubum *(bottom left)*. | COOKING A MEAL in the camp near Kubum *(bottom right)*.

A DISPLACED MOTHER and child in the Dereig camp outside Nyala. Do they have hope that the world will respond to their plight and help end the conflict in Darfur? | A WOMAN PUTS on the common garment worn by women throughout Darfur, in the wind in the Dereig Camp for internally displaced persons. Whereas men's clothing is often white, women in Darfur take pride in their colorful clothing.

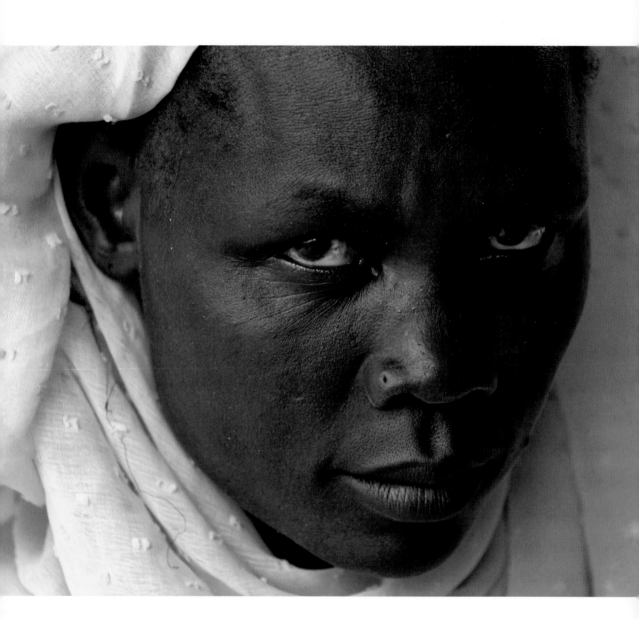

A DISPLACED WOMAN in the
Dereig camp, waiting for peace.

Perhaps it is telling that these two respected leaders were once in politics. In 1997, Messinger, then Manhattan Borough president, failed to unseat Rudolph Giuliani as mayor of New York. Edgar, a six-term congressman from Pennsylvania, lost a Senate race to incumbent Arlen Specter. Subsequently, he led the National Council of Churches and now is president of the government watchdog group Common Cause.

Like their secular counterparts in the Darfur activist community, both Messinger and Edgar have been frustrated by the continued intransigence of the Sudanese government and a lack of substantive response by the United States. "We weren't completely effective but we weren't completely a failure, either," Edgar said of the faith community. "I think the success came in speaking to power and spreading the word. The failure was in not getting governments or the UN to respond effectively." Messinger was even blunter: "We haven't been successful because the killings continue," she said. "It's frustrating. The broader efforts, of trying to end the violence in Darfur, have not yet succeeded." She noted that historically, activist movements such as the antiwar protests of the 1960s and 1970s took time. "And of course, with Darfur, time is exactly what you don't have."

Both Messinger and Edgar believe the United States has been too distracted by the war in Iraq to do much about Darfur. International alienation about U.S. foreign policy made for a sure-fire failure, the two leaders agreed. Edgar said disdainfully, "I gave up Bush, Cheney, and Rumsfeld for Lent. That gang set their sights first on Afghanistan and then Iraq." He added, "The U.S. put our eggs in two baskets, Afghanistan and Iraq, and then drained away any potential for a response in Darfur." Edgar was not suggesting he would have supported a unilateral U.S. intervention in Darfur. But an early, multilateral action would have been appropriate and might have worked, he argued. A similar response in Rwanda might have saved as many as four hundred thousand victims of that genocide. As for the humanitarian response in Darfur, Edgar praised what had been accomplished, but wondered if there could have been more done to protect those within the camps. "Even with the refugee and displacement camps, we didn't do enough to be sure the camps were protected," he said. "This was a silent tsunami—out of sight."

Edgar felt that activists and others probably expected too much when U.S. officials, first Powell and later Bush himself, called the events in Darfur genocide. After all, the UN charter says that "if you name it genocide, you're obliged to act." Edgar believes that in hindsight, activists made a mistake in not taking more visible action—such as more embassy protests. "We didn't take it to the next level and I think, in retrospect, we needed to ratchet up the civil disobedience. These are our brothers and sisters we let die." Personally, Edgar claims his own arrest outside the Sudanese embassy during a 2004 protest as a badge of honor. "I have four arrests for civil obedience and five honorary doctorates; I'm now looking for the fifth arrest."

Edgar believes the American Jewish community is the clear leader among faith groups involved in Darfur activism—as the grandfather of three Jewish children (one of

Edgar's sons married a Jewish woman), Edgar was struck by the high visibility given to Darfur concerns when he visited his grandchildren's Arlington, Virginia, synagogue. He contrasts this with what he feels is a tendency among some U.S. Christian leaders and clergy to be too embedded in denominational politics and concerns to speak out about issues like Darfur—though certainly many churches, including some in Edgar's own denomination, have vigorously worked on the cause of Darfur. (Perhaps most famously, the Ginghamsburg United Methodist Church in Tipp City, Ohio, has embarked on a five-year, multimillion-dollar effort to raise funds for Darfur humanitarian assistance.) A nagging problem for the U.S. faith community, Edgar said, is that "we're generically nice, and in the U.S., we have the added burden of being comfortable." In general, Darfur has not been "a hard sell" for Christian communities to embrace because "the stories from Darfur are similar to biblical stories about oppression and unnecessary death that run from Exodus to the narratives of Jesus' crucifixion," Edgar said. Even so, the former congressman believes more could have been done, and mentions his own guilt in not traveling to Darfur as part of a delegation that included Messinger. "We need to be more aggressive in bearing witness," he said.

"Look at the Old Testament and the New Testament. The prophets never had a majority before acting and speaking out," he said. "But it's always those courageous remnants that change the world: those small, courageous remnants." Edgar's own denomination was evidence of the various kinds of Darfur response: on the one hand, The United Methodist Church's General Board of Church and Society, an advocacy group, worked with the ENOUGH Project on producing a study guide for Christian action on ending genocide in Darfur; on the other, the UMC's global mission and humanitarian divisions proscribed the use of the word "genocide" in reference to Darfur out of concern for the safety of their Darfur programs and workers.

Messinger mentioned those "remnants," Jewish tradition and the historical legacy that has grounded her organization's work on Darfur. "Jews are obligated to respond to poverty and oppression," Messinger affirmed, citing *tikkun olam*, the Jewish mandate to heal the world. "If Jews don't respond vociferously," she said, "then we're living the lie of our own history." Messenger noted that too often, the phrase "never again" has come to mean, as David Rieff has put it, that "'never again' will Germans kill Jews in Europe in the 1940s." Messinger said, "That is *not* what the words mean."

Some have made, and others have questioned, the comparisons between the Holocaust and Darfur. For her part, Messinger cited Elie Wiesel's belief that the Holocaust is its own reality and experience, a world event that doesn't allow other comparisons. In fact, she states, the argument about genocide and Darfur is not made on the basis of any comparison to the Holocaust. Messinger herself was surprised when she read the UN Convention on the Prevention and Punishment of the Crime of Genocide, which clearly defines genocide as "any effort to kill all or part of a people."

"You almost get the feeling that al-Bashir got out the convention and said, 'OK, we can do this, we can do that. Darfur meets the UN convention's definition. Calling something genocide doesn't take away anything from the Holocaust." As for any comparison of al-Bashir in Darfur to a visit by Hitler to the death camps, Messinger said: "I wouldn't make the comparison; the comparison would get you into a heap of trouble. I think what Bashir did was simply based on the ICC action and the fact that he felt he needed to put on a 'good-time' show."

"Will It Make Any Difference?"

Five years into the conflict, some grassroots Darfur activists in churches and synagogues were feeling tired. "People want to do something about Darfur but don't feel the leadership is coming from the UN or from Washington," said Carl Sayres, a software architect in Summit, New Jersey. "They're genuinely interested but don't have the tools to do much about it." Sayres, thirty-five, was among those trying to equip churches and synagogues in Summit with the tools. He is an organizer and spokesman of Summit's Darfur Genocide Rescue Committee—a grassroots, interfaith coalition "established to educate and inspire people to act in peaceful ways to facilitate an end to the conflict in Darfur and convey a compassionate presence and hope to the people of Darfur." Its members' religious affiliations were representative of several faith streams within the movement—Jewish, Unitarian, and Christian.

Among the group's successes was an interfaith Thanksgiving service that normally attracts fifty and ended up garnering four hundred when a Darfur theme was introduced in 2007. "That was an unheard-of turnout," said Sayres, who worships at the Summit Jewish Community Center. He was looking for something optimistic he could bring back to his group when he attended a 2008 Labor Day week event at the Jewish Community Center in Manhattan, presented by the New York Center for Conflict Dialogue and billed as a discussion on peace and reconciliation in Darfur. The draw was a scheduled appearance by Abdalmahmood Abdalhaleem Mohamad, a representative of the Sudanese Mission to the United Nations, and Sayres said any good news he could glean from the evening would be welcome. "The more optimistic I can be, the more successful I can be. If the situation is hopeless, people won't get involved," he said, acknowledging, however, that a "growing sense of hopelessness" was setting in among some activists.

Given the powerful sentiments the government of Sudan can evoke, I had images of protests outside the JCC. There were none, but an email "blast" for the event did, according to a JCC staff member, elicit some angry responses. Still, it turned out to be a quiet, even staid affair, with Mohamad not even showing up—an event organizer said preparations for the upcoming UN General Assembly had kept the envoy away.

Other Darfur activists in the audience—some of whom could only attend part of the evening because the monthly meeting of the New York City Coalition for Darfur was planned for the same evening at a nearby United Methodist church—shared some of

Sayres's concerns. I had just read a piece coauthored by Chad Hazlett, one of the genocide activists I had met, suggesting that "activism for Darfur was distorted by having learned the 'wrong lesson' from Rwanda." That lesson, Hazlett and his coauthor argued, was the belief that by merely calling what was happening in Darfur a genocide—a clear victory for activists—"a policy to stop it would follow." Hazlett said, "Once again, people had fallen into the trap of viewing a current genocide through the lens of an earlier one."

"That's a fair criticism," said Sharon Silber, director of the New York City Coalition for Darfur. "We know now that it's not enough just to make noise." Silber also agreed with Bob Edgar's argument that the Darfur activism might not have been vocal enough. "Our noise hasn't had enough sting to it," she agreed, though she also acknowledged that a certain frustration had set in. "People are sick of hearing about it, and there's a kind of helplessness setting in."

The man chosen to debate the no-show mission representative was Simon Deng, a southern Sudanese and one of the strongest critics of the Khartoum regime living in the United States. It was an open question whether his presentation gave the New York activists hope or more reason to be pessimistic about Darfur. Deng, an impressive, impassionate speaker, is best known for his advocacy in ending slavery in southern Sudan, though he said his activism stems "not because I am southern Sudanese but because I am Sudanese." Still, he repeatedly returned to the theme that the problem *of* Darfur did not begin *with* Darfur—the government of Sudan's response to Darfur, he argued, was simply a continuation of government policy in southern Sudan. While not minimizing what had happened in Darfur, Deng felt that the issue of genocide could have been properly applied to the south and had not been, at least by the United States, the African Union, or what he called "The United Do-Nothing Nations."

"It became a ruthless war never before seen in Africa," Deng said of the North-South conflict, "and Khartoum got away with it because no one raised their voice." (He did not mention the outcry by the U.S. evangelical Christian community.) Militias like the *Janjaweed* were used in the south; the government, as in Darfur, had called what occurred in the south simply "lawlessness." The government embrace of "Arab" identity politics had done grievous harm, setting Khartoum against other parts of the country. "Islam has been used in Sudan as a weapon," he said. Deng also harshly criticized China and Russia, given their ties to Sudan, as the "biggest obstacles to peace in Darfur and in Sudan." He left the audience with a mixed message: on the one hand, he said recent news indicated that the North-South peace accord was fraying, and if the trend continued, "that could dwarf Darfur, inflaming the entire region." As a corollary, he added peace in one region could help peace in another, but war in one area in Sudan would likely make war in another more tenable. Deng put the onus of the problems facing Sudan on its leaders, whom he did not describe favorably. "When you say, 'That's a light,'" he said, pointing to the ceiling, "Khartoum will say, 'It's not a light.' That's how they act."

While he acknowledged that activists "are still beating the drums but the killing continues," he urged his fellow activists not to give up. He even seemed touched by the care and attention those in the audience were showing about a country few had ever visited. "You're taking the time for this issue. This has affected you."

At the end of the evening, a JCC staffer said the audience "had come expecting a word of hope from a politician and you got more bad news from an activist." Carl Sayres, the New Jersey activist, acknowledged the pessimism, saying, "This is the frustration a lot of activists are feeling. If we do this for another five years, will it make any difference?" He added, "I'm going to speak at my Rosh Hashanah service to seven hundred people; I'm not naïve but if I'm going to promote this, I want them to feel it's worth it. I think that hope is very important; to mobilize people and get them to act you have to tell people that their efforts are not in vain, that their efforts are meaningful. I'm looking for sources of hope and inspiration." Did he find them that night in Deng's presentation? He was honest, if tactful. "I was expecting a more hopeful message tonight." Sayres paused, and then acknowledged that the work needed to continue. "There is evil in the world. We know this. It rears its head whenever we're not on our guard," he said. "However hopeless it is, we can't let our guard down and say, 'It won't work' because that's when evil really flourishes." Was this a particularly Jewish issue? "It's a Jewish issue because of the Holocaust, but it can't *just* be a Jewish issue; it has to be the world's issue. Obviously, Jews have a very strong feeling for it."

Had there been any success? Sayres thought there had been, yes: "Speaking out has certainly slowed it down," he said of the killing in Darfur. "If al-Bashir had not had this pressure, he might have killed as many as 2.5 million. Speaking up has made a difference. It's better than if we had done nothing." He paused again. "Look—at a fundamental level, if we look the other way and don't get involved, that's when the evil will do what it wants."

❖   ❖   ❖

In the spring of 2005, I learned that things had improved for Um Seifa and Labado, the areas I had visited that been attacked. In fact, Labado had became the base for a contingent of African Union peacekeepers from Nigeria, Malawi, and Namibia. The security offered by the AU gave a safe haven for returning residents who had fled earlier. And in late May 2005, Labado had a visitor: then-United Nations Secretary-General Kofi Annan. One European humanitarian official told Annan's visiting party of the need for a stronger protection mandate for the AU peacekeepers—"Security is still the main issue," she said.

That was a reference to the fact that the small African Union force then deployed in Darfur had a limited mandate in which it could only monitor and report human rights violations. The decision by the UN in 2007 to allow a more robust force of twenty-six thousand allowed a slightly expanded mandate—granting the right to use force in protecting civilians. However, the peacekeepers were still encumbered by not having authorization to actually take weapons from belligerent forces.

The Sudanese villagers who were not able to meet the dignitaries plainly made their wishes known to Annan. In a gesture that would have cheered the Darfur activists in Summit, New Jersey, they held aloft signs that read: "Bring us peace in Darfur."

❖　　　❖　　　❖

Wrestling with Reconciliation

The attempt to face down evil through activism—whether successful or not—has been only a portion of the faith community's work around Darfur. Much of the humanitarian efforts that have fed and schooled those in the displacement camps of both Darfur and neighboring Chad is due to the work of relief groups with religious ties—Christian, Jewish, Muslim. One part of that endeavor deserves special mention because it has not been widely heralded—the struggle to bring about reconciliation among warring factions and between groups and parties that have been victimized and aggrieved.

Reconciliation is a sensitive topic, as some survivors do not want to contemplate it, given the horrific trauma they have experienced. Reconciliation is also tricky because of the *nature* of the violence itself. Human rights violation and violence perpetuated as political acts wound people not only physically, economically, psychologically, and spiritually, but also because survivors "have been violated by those supposed to protect them. The political adds a deep injustice," said Daniel Philpott, who teaches at the Joan B. Kroc Institute for International Peace Studies at the University of Notre Dame. "It compounds the brute suffering."

Oftentimes, the woundedness is compounded because governments will either forget or lie about what they have done. "Victims will often say: I haven't been recognized. It feels like a redoubling of the violation, in not being seen or heard or recognized. And of course, when others in your community have also been aggrieved, you identify with that people, you fight for revenge. People have deep identities with their communities. That's what makes us human."

The passage of time, without overt displays or efforts of reconciliation, can sometimes help the process of reconciliation. Over several generations, Japan's relations with the United States have improved despite few concrete displays of reconciliation on either side, Philpott argues. But "putting things right" with a community's sense of woundedness can occur with the participation of religious groups and leaders—a fact Philpott believes is often overlooked or minimized by secular human rights activists and humanitarians.

Even religious outsiders—at least those who respect the religious mores and traditions of an affected group—can command respect, Philpott said. "Religious leaders can tap into resources—ritualistic, textual—that command rich ideas and tradition and have real potential for making a difference."

One of the ways this can happen is by recognizing how reconciliation is embedded in the Abrahamic traditions of Christianity, Islam, and Judaism. "People need help to see that reconciliation is embedded in their own faith and can be a resource for peace and conflict resolution." John Prendergast has suggested that such attempts at peace and reconciliation may have their place in Darfur, but that these efforts are a bit "like trying to play baseball in a football field." In other words, the scale of violence is so massive that traditional tribal councils and other forums are not the places where the work of peace and healing can occur.

Philpott said it is true that the "morally rich traditions of reconciliation within tribal cultures for, say, stealing a cow" may not have application for a Darfur. Yet, he said, small-scale efforts, if done often enough, *can* have an effect. "It's hard to generalize," he said, but in Mozambique, which experienced a nearly two-decades civil war that ended in 1992, "there were widespread uses of ritual and reconciliation; the Catholic Church was involved in those. These efforts could make a difference if there were enough of them. Obviously, if it's only one village involved, it doesn't help the larger setting. But even if it's regional, it's possible it can do good."

"Sometimes reconciliation is seen as utopian, and someone could justifiably ask: does this ever really happen?" Philpott said. "Yet there are partial successes: places like South Africa, Chile, and East Timor, where people have embraced reconciliation. This has been, can be, and is, a concrete political practice."

✦   ✦   ✦

Could it happen in Darfur?

One of the largest humanitarian efforts in Darfur—an ecumenical operation involving major Catholic and Protestant relief networks—has tried to advance peace and reconciliation by fostering better communication between Arab and African communities. The work has centered on admittedly small undertakings such as exchange visits and training conflict resolution committees to negotiate small-scale accords and equip paralegals to advocate for women who have survived sexual assault. These accords include efforts at guaranteeing unhindered access to a water well or the ability to travel safely to a local market. As my coauthor Paul Jeffrey noted in a 2007 report, "Such daily improvements bridge the ethnic tensions that the government has taken advantage of in its militarization of the region."

Another example is from the town of Kabum, where a local reconciliation committee helped mediate a violent dispute between two Arab groups—farmers and herders. (The so-called Arab-African divide is not the only source of bitter dispute within Darfur.) Adam Ateem, the project's director of peace-building and protection, told Jeffrey that the committee, which included members of African tribes, successfully mediated between Arab farmers and herders and worked out an amicable solution.

Ateem, who studied law in Khartoum, said tribal allegiances are deep-rooted in Darfur and in all of Sudan, and can be a hindrance to resolving conflicts. He has former law school classmates who are members of the Janjaweed. *"I ran into this old friend one day, and I asked him why if he was so well-educated that he had chosen to support the militias," Ateem told Jeffrey. "He talked to me about his need to support his father and his tribe over everything else, even if the government is going to use them to take everything away from the Africans and give it to the Arabs."*

"We've got to change this way of thinking."

5

Facing the Future

Grievous wrongdoing doesn't just wound the body and soul, and it doesn't just worm its way into our identity. It also entraps us. Like a ball chained to a prisoner's leg, it drags heavily on our spirit, and prevents it from roaming freely, stretching itself into the unknown, playing with new possibilities, imagining alternative futures.

— Miroslav Volf, *The End of Memory: Remembering Rightly in a Violent World* (2006)

Old ways of thinking and doing are likely to be the norm in Darfur for the foreseeable future. The signs, not surprisingly, range from discouraging to potentially ominous. Five years of activist work, diplomatic pressure, and attempts at peacemaking have yielded some successes, but few tangible results for those who have survived Darfur's violence. There may be fragments of hope, but the operative word is fragments, not hope. The narrative in Darfur keeps changing on the ground, with increasing layers of complexity and chaos. But the narrative at the top continues to hold: the international community has aligned itself with *the idea* of the responsibility to protect civilians from genocide, but the idea has not cost anyone much. Those paying the price of continued violence are Darfuris themselves.

In a commendably frank admission, reported by Maggie Farley of the *Los Angeles Times*, Jan Eliasson, the one-time UN envoy to Darfur, acknowledged in June 2008 that the prognosis for Darfur was not good. As Farley reported:

> When Jan Eliasson agreed to be a U.N. envoy to Darfur, he believed peace for the beleaguered region of Sudan was within reach. But after

18 months of shuttle diplomacy, rebel groups are more fractured and violent than ever and the Sudanese government is again engaged in brutal attacks on villages, he told the Security Council on Tuesday.

The chance for peace has slipped away for now, he told the council "with much regret," and the focus must revert to restoring security. He scolded all parties in the conflict, including the Security Council and himself, for not doing more to halt the violence....

"For over five years, millions of people have suffered enormously," said Eliasson, a former president of the General Assembly and once Sweden's foreign minister. "This simply can't go on."

The deployment of U.N. and African Union troops to the region has lagged alarmingly because of Sudanese government obstructions, U.N. bureaucracy and lack of equipment from donor nations, said Eliasson, but the goal of having 16,000 peacekeepers on the ground by year's end now seems on track.

No matter how many more peacekeepers are sent, both the displaced and humanitarian workers in Darfur are skeptical about how much, ultimately, the peacekeepers can do, particularly given a limited mandate. A similar, though smaller operation with the backing of the European Union has failed to stem the tide of violence in neighboring Chad—violence attributed mostly to banditry and lawlessness created by war between rebel factions that are attacking Chad from bases in Darfur. Seasoned aid workers roll their eyes as they say a one-year operation in Chad is nearly meaningless. Why? "It will take them nine months to learn how to drive in the desert. It's not serious," one said.

Unfortunately, Eliasson's striking plea, "This simply can't go on," has been turned on its head. What *has* happened is likely to *continue to happen* for some time. During a visit to Chad in 2008, officials of relief agencies working with refugees in Darfur and Chad told me that the displaced could still be in camps five, ten, or conceivably, even twenty years from now if conditions on the ground do not improve. These camps are becoming permanent features of Darfur's and Chad's brutalized and blighted landscape.

Such predictions, admittedly and notoriously risky, are based on objective, even quantifiable realities and are related to the issue of security. Those who have been displaced fear the continued violence within Darfur. Several problems are referenced by Eliasson. The lumbering international response is marked by indifference and confusion. The Sudanese government has shown little commitment to ending the violence and has even begun a new campaign of violence within Darfur. In August 2008, Sudanese security forces, citing the presence of armed rebels at the Kalma displacement camp, killed thirty-one people, including women and children. That prompted condemnation from a United Nations official but not much else. The obdurate Darfur rebels, particularly Abdul Wahid

Mohammad al-Nur's faction, have dug in with no sign of compromise, saying they will not negotiate with the Sudanese government until the day-to-day security environment in Darfur improves. Ongoing factional violence between, among, and within the rebel and allied paramilitary groups continues, making returns to villages impossible.

There are at least three other reasons why those who have been displaced may not return. Two of them can be termed worrisome because they show the seeming durability of the conflict: the expansion of the Darfur conflict into a regional conflagration that includes Chad, and despite the efforts of faith groups and others, the continued challenge of possible reconciliation between those victimized by the violence and those they say perpetuated it. A third reason is more neutral, but it too shows the persistence of violence as a bringer of change. Displacement *itself* is changing those who have survived and must ultimately rebuild their lives anew.

Darfur's Other War: Chad

Over and over, I heard people in the Chadian capital of N'Djamena say that the war in Chad is essentially the same as the war in Darfur. "It's the same conflict, the same region, affecting the same people" became something of a three-part refrain. The quick explanation for this was that the events in Darfur were simply spilling over into Chad. While there is some truth to that, it is also an oversimplification, as analyst Jerome Tubiana cautioned in a 2008 study published by the Swiss-based research group Small Arms Survey. "Khartoum and N'Djamena have been engaged in an on-again, off-again proxy conflict using one another's rebel movements since the Darfur conflict began in 2003, most intensively since 2005," Tubiana wrote. "Khartoum has attempted on multiple occasions to unify Chadian rebel groups to destabilize or even overthrow the Déby regime." (Idriss Déby, an army lieutenant general, came to power in Chad during a 1990 military coup. A member of the Zaghawa tribe, he has added the name "Itno"— warrior—to his surname.)

In fact, the conflict goes back much further than that and can be at least partially traced to another war—that between Libya and Chad over a territorial dispute. In 1987, that war spilled over into Darfur. Colonel Muammar Gaddafi, bent at the time on regional domination, in fact used Darfur "as a rear base, and flooded Darfur with automatic weapons, advertised the impotence of local government, and brought an ideology of Arab supremacism," Alex de Waal wrote in the *ACAS Bulletin*. "In response, the Fur organized village defense groups. It became a Darfurian civil war."

So, in fact, the war in Darfur might be said to have roots *in* Chad. But what of now? De Waal, among others, has suggested that Darfur has actually "become part of a regional nexus of conflict" that includes both countries, "characterized by a political pattern in which both local elites (tribal chiefs, militia commanders, small-town political leaders) and followers (especially armed young men) have contingent loyalties, constantly engaged in political bargaining with their actual and potential patrons in Khartoum, Tripoli and (more recently) N'Djamena."

In short, Chad and Darfur are now a single entity—geographically, ethnically, linguistically—with an artificial border, the result of colonial history. (While Sudan was under British rule, Chad was under French control.) This border, *le ligne rouge* (the "red line"), is becoming ever more dangerous as the boundaries evaporate and become a zone of military and rebel activity, refugee crossings, and banditry. Adding to this lethal mix is that many believe some of the tension between Chad and Sudan is due to personal animus between Presidents Déby and al-Bashir. This entanglement had become, by many accounts, a personal tit for tat between the two leaders. It does not take very long to see the results of this jostling in Chad. In a startling February 2008 incursion into the Chadian capital, rebels supported by al-Bashir were unable to dislodge Déby. Three months later, evidence of the fierce battle was still visible. Bullet casings and shrapnel still littered the city's sidewalks; bullet holes pockmarked numerous storefronts; the sound of French fighter jets occasionally punctuated the air. Perhaps most perplexing was the sad evidence of Déby's forces cutting down trees along the city's main thoroughfares to prevent rebels from using them as sniper posts. Where once stately trees grew, now decidedly unstately tree trunks stand.

Despite these obvious signs of trouble, Chadians and foreigners seemed to take the difficulties in stride. (The small cadre of internationals in Chad are of two basic types: humanitarian workers and oil company representatives. Jets flying from Paris to N'Djamena have expanded first-class service to accommodate oil company workers; the humanitarian workers sit in the back.) But foreigners and Chadians acted as if they had seen it all before and would, most likely, see it all again before too long. And they did: in June 2008, rebels sacked the town of Goz Beida, a key humanitarian hub and a headquarters for UN work in eastern Chad.

Outsiders are fond of saying that Chadians (and by implication, Darfuris) are a warrior people. They suggest that violence is an essential element of the national character. Said one humanitarian worker, "These guys are really tough. Déby is like Napoleon Bonaparte at the front. He's a fighter." One rumor making the rounds in Chad had Déby traveling yearly to France to renew his fighter pilot's license. The statement of another aid worker, whose agency helps child soldiers return to their former lives, startled me. I asked if the youngsters feel any remorse in the course of the program. "This is a culture of warriors," he said, "so there's nothing to feel guilty about."

Whether or not you accept the "essentialist argument" that this part of the world is somehow "prone" to violence (and I do not), it is clear that any solution to the problems in Darfur must take Chad into account. Jaap Aantjes, who until May 2008 served as the Lutheran World Federation country director in Chad, has had heated discussions with colleagues in Darfur about the situation in both countries. While not for a moment minimizing Darfur's tragedy, he believes the international community needs to realize that the problems of Darfur can no longer be viewed in isolation. "I've said, 'Don't put all your eggs into the one basket of Darfur.' The Darfur problem is a regional problem." He added, "You can't look only at the 'center' (Darfur itself). You also have to respond at the edges, not just in the center." Doing so was going to remain difficult, Aantjes told me, because, "it's obvious that it's become a personal war between the leaders of Sudan and Chad. In both cases, war is taken to the streets, to the other side's cities."

One afternoon I spoke with a West African aid worker, as he and a group of colleagues waited in N'Djamena during a moment when, due to security restrictions, travel to the border areas of eastern Chad had been halted. He spoke warily, but evenly, pointing to "elasticity of demand," or a "demand curve": the leaders of Chad and Sudan each "want more—more power, more allies—and are now trying to destabilize the other." In each case, the Sudanese and Chadian leaders were using ethnic tension for personal revenge.

One characteristic of this battle was unusual, particularly given the reports of attacks on the displaced in the camps in Darfur. Anti-Déby rebels respected the relief agency's independent status, and there had actually been few attacks on the displaced themselves in Chad. This was small comfort to those affected, as the fighting between rebels in Chad left them no choice but to flee their villages. In Darfur, humanitarian workers inevitably came up against Sudanese government intransigence and bureaucratic snafus. Given the extremes of poverty, climate, the proliferation of small arms and security, working in Chad—though immensely difficult—was easier in at least one sense: relief groups and the government cooperated fairly well, though relations were marred in 2007 after the government of Chad charged a French charity, Zoé's Ark, with child abduction. (The charity claimed the 103 children under its care were Darfur refugees, but it was later determined most were from Chad.)

Still, even if this war within Chad was conducted "honorably," it had created an environment in which general lawlessness and impunity were able to flourish. The biggest threat to relief groups and to those living in the camps, this African aid worker said, were not the rebel groups but roaming bandits, looking for guns, cars, and victims for ransom. It was becoming increasingly difficult to distinguish the bandits from the rebels from the military. Moreover, "when the government priority is in fighting rebels, things like the humanitarian situation become less of a priority," said one humanitarian worker in pointed understatement. Moreover, if the Chadian government could not match the government of Sudan's in sheer mendacity, its disregard for the plight of its own citizens was apparent in nearly every other way. If the wider Darfur area "is one of the most dangerous areas in the world, the poverty (in Chad) is flagrant," the worker said.

A Potent Mix of Violence and Disorder

If trying to make sense of the conflict was not always easy, assessing the conflict's results on the ground is more tangible. Christophe Droeven, Catholic Relief Services' country representative to Chad, compared the "far east" of Chad to the U.S. Wild West of a century ago. Ethnic tensions in Chad and Darfur heightened a tense situation of ethnic conflict in eastern Chad, resulting in "general impunity." Where there is no system of justice, there is "no border," or "frame," in which issues of conflict can be resolved. In such an environment, Droeven said, people are no longer under a traditional legal or social system, and it is easy, in particular, for "young people to acquire Kalashnikovs."

Indeed, the problem of child soldiers was a part of a potent mix of violence and disorder that marks Chad: I heard similar "Darfur" stories in Chad—of villages destroyed and people displaced, repeated stories of sexual violence against women. A feeling of chaos and insecurity seemed the norm. Still, in the midst of robberies or landmines, overworked and underpaid humanitarian workers, nearly all of them African, did their committed best to salve the poor living conditions in camps where the displaced lamented their state of perpetual limbo. Were they staying? Returning? They did not know. Conditions in the camps for the displaced in Chad were probably the worst I have seen anywhere, including Darfur. What lingers in the memory, aside from the debilitating extremes of heat, are the chaotic camp layouts. At the beginning of the rainy season, flooding created the constant open-air exposure to mud and water as well as to insects the size of cell phones. Malaria was a constant concern, as were other water-borne diseases.

Some of the poor conditions, it has to be said, were due to the fact that the arrivals to the camps were fairly recent. In contrast, the Darfur refugees in Chad were fairly well-established, having been in camps since 2004 or so. Unfortunately, the humanitarian response for the internally displaced persons (IDPs in humanitarian parlance) within Chad has not been as well-funded or well-publicized as the plight of the Darfur refugees. Under international covenants, the Darfur refugees are entitled to more humanitarian assistance than the IDPs because they have crossed an international border. This anomaly caused no end of frustration and protest by the IDPs who repeatedly pointed out that they were survivors of essentially the same conflict. Humanitarian workers understood the frustration, but added that they were powerless to change the rules in place. The justification for the difference goes like this: when refugees cross an international border, they are in legal limbo and can't return easily to their native countries; the internally displaced, in theory anyway, are in a better position to find safer places because they are in their own country. If the same amount of assistance is given to the internally displaced, it is argued, large numbers of the internally displaced may move simply to receive assistance.

✦   ✦   ✦

One of those unhappy about this "hierarchy" of aid assistance was Haroun Abdallah, seventy-eight, a village elder. He said the aid situation was only one of a host of problems he had to face since leaving his village. For one thing, it had proven difficult to keep his village intact given the casualities the Janjaweed *had inflicted: two hundred dead from a village of twenty-five hundred; five days of walking to get to the displacement site, an eighty-kilometer trip; a remnant of about fifty people now lived together in the displacement camp. The contrast between life then and now was stark. I met Abdallah on the cusp of the rainy season and at the end of the planting season, a particularly difficult and anxious time for the displaced. Their former lives were based on the seasonal cycles of planting and harvest. "When we were in the village, we lacked for nothing," he said, adding that in the violence that overtook the village, the villagers' horses, camels, and other livestock were left behind. "We want to go back but we can't," he said. "Our enemies are there. If we returned, the* Janjaweed *would attack us. They were fully armed, and we only had bow and arrows. How can you fight if you only have bow and arrows? That's why we had to leave." What about their relations with those he called "Arabs"? He said that historically, the Arab and non-Arab tribes have enjoyed good relations. But since the attack—going on two years now—"if we see an Arab, we're afraid. It's difficult." Did he have any thoughts of revenge? Abdallah hedged. His goal was to keep what remained of his village intact. "We'll leave everything else in the hands of God."*

❖   ❖   ❖

Abdallah's statement could be read in several different ways—was he suggesting peace or revenge? That was a notable ambiguity that humanitarian workers wrestle with daily. Diallo M'bemba, a Guinean who works with Lutheran World Federation (LWF) in eastern Chad, notes that the situation in Darfur and Chad is now sufficiently deep-rooted (with problems dating back decades) and widespread (with millions who have experienced bombings, rape, and other acts of violence) that for "someone to expect to reconcile like that," he said, snapping his fingers, is "very, very difficult." Look at Chad, a country that has essentially been mired in conflict for thirty years and is awash in weapons. One cannot expect peace to break out in such an environment, he said. "Yes, they want to reconcile," he added, "and perhaps people, deep down in their hearts, want that. Perhaps it will happen. But these conflicts have been going on so long, with root causes so deep...." His voice trailed off, shaking his head. "Forgive and forget? It won't work like that."

Still, M'bemba believes reconciliation must be a goal—if for no other reason than for the sheer pragmatism of improving day-to-day life. He agrees with his LWF colleague Esther Isaac who said, "If people have a problem and it's not dealt with, it ends up being another pathology." Isaac knows something of this firsthand. Isaac, forty-five, a native of Sierra Leone and the mother of three children, is a notably passionate advocate for the displaced, particularly women. That is partly due to her own family history, which includes bouts of displacement from several conflicts in West Africa. Isaac's mother was a displaced Liberian, and her family had to move from war-torn Sierra Leone to neighboring Guinea. "I can empathize with them," Isaac said of the displaced. "I know it's not a normal situation. They come to the camps with nothing." At one point I saw Isaac assist a woman at a food distribution center whose bullying, estranged husband nearly cost the woman her food rations. (Isaac was successful: the woman got her food.) Isaac often expressed exasperation about the sexual inequality in the camps, which ranges from outright sexual violence against women to the unfair distribution and scale of work. "Men," Isaac said, shaking her head. "This issue of sexual violence is very serious. Women have no voice, no rights."

To Isaac, the only way to put an end to these and other pathologies is to start building communities that, at the least, reject violence and move toward reconciliation. This is done in part by empowering individuals and communities that have experienced violence and have lost an individual or collective sense of dignity. It is not an easy task for a host of reasons, including the fact that women, in particular, are not likely to come forward and reveal hidden experiences such as rape, which Isaac firmly believes—as do prominent UN humanitarian officials—is used as an act of war. "Women tend to hide in the shadows," she said.

By contrast, Isaac believes men recover more easily from trauma—in part because of their positions of power. Even so, she said, men tend to react by drinking and taking drugs, addictions that can grow into problems for others. Of course, ex-combatants have their own traumas to face. Esther knows an ex-soldier who "killed another man to drink blood because he was so thirsty. Now he's totally traumatized." If these individual issues aren't addressed at first, they eventually become community issues—pathologies in which acts of violence can be perpetuated. So-called "psycho-social" programs address issues of "mind, soul, and body" both individually and in the social setting. "You have to react with the community. It's a community issue," Isaac said, adding, "But it takes time, it takes time."

Gender Roles: Broadening but Not Shifting

The passage of time may be one element in the process of healing; an unresolved issue is that of gender roles. "It's very striking, the amount of practical day-to-day labor women do in the camps," said Susan M. St. Ville, a trauma and gender specialist at the University of Notre Dame's Kroc Center. Her work in northern Uganda—another zone of conflict in East Africa—found similar patterns to those in Chad and Darfur.

Without job opportunities, men struggle, become depressed, turn to drink, and cannot see hope for the future. By contrast, women often find their horizons broadened by camp educational activities, but they are still burdened with having to earn an income and perform the domestic work of caring for family. "The gender roles are being broadened but not shifting. The men can't conceive of taking on different roles, so the women are left doing most of the work," St. Ville said. "It's a real gender mess." Given the attention by humanitarian groups to women, a kind of backlash begins to emerge by men who are shamed by their new situations—rates of domestic violence increase, as do separations, divorces, and family divisions. "Violence, alcoholism, and depression—they go together," she said, raising the difficult question of how humanitarian assistance is received. "I think our models come out of what is just and needed, but they are brought into a culture where there is no groundwork or foundation for changing gender roles."

As for the issue of trauma, St. Ville said that her experiences in working with trauma counselors in Africa have convinced her—and in contrast to Isaac's belief—that it is women, and not men, who are generally more resilient. Some of that, St. Ville theorizes, is due to the continuation of expected gender roles—that of having and raising children. Women "feel they have a purpose: their families. Yes, it can be burdensome, but it's linked to resilience and purpose." By contrast, men, having lost their economic role, can feel alienated and apart from their families as they try to recover from their own trauma.

Women's resilience may also have something to do with their comfort in expressing their pain and seeking community. If women hide in the shadows, as Isaac said they do, they are at least not alone *in* the shadows—men tend to keep their experiences hidden within themselves. "It can *seem* like women are experiencing the pain more deeply," St. Ville said, "but they heal better because they seek community and the community—which is often a community of other women—accepts their expression of emotion.

"It is striking how much better women do psychologically than men."

Still, men have not experienced rape, and St. Ville finds the issue of sexual violence enormously complicated, in part because women in camps who have survived rape are keenly aware that the outside world perceives, even conceptualizes, places like Darfur or northern Uganda "as regions, or zones, of trauma."

I told St. Ville that during my second trip to Darfur I was struck by the kind of communal identity, complete with a common narrative, that women had embraced as survivors of rape. She said that was a common experience. "They have managed to have a comfort with the narrative; that's good," she said, recalling listening to stories by rape survivors in Uganda. "But sometimes, hearing the stories with my counselor ears, I felt I wasn't hearing the deepest level of the trauma." Sometimes the expression—the storytelling—she said, does not capture the real internal reality rape survivors are feeling. They will recite a narrative that "does allow for a connection—between survivors and people on the outside." But that narrative often does not quite capture the horror of what they have experienced. Sometimes "you just get the sense that people are reading from a script… telling the story without affect…. There is a lot to be captured that the story can't capture because the experiences are so really horrible."

As for the larger issues of reconciliation, St. Ville cautioned that outsiders should be careful—reconciliation must be something that is organic and comes from within, not from without, a community. Humanitarian aid groups must be careful that their needs—donors' needs—for reconciliation do not overpower the needs of those actually doing the reconciling. "Who is given the power to assent to reconciliation or not—that's a very big question. My feeling is that a just reconciliation is what the survivors of trauma determine it is." This is no easy matter, in part because sometimes what is called "reconciliation" is actually a kind of nostalgia for a culture that either never was or a dream of something that will never exist again. "I wouldn't say reconciliation isn't possible," St. Ville said. "But what kind of shape does it take under these very difficult situations?"

◆   ◆   ◆

Stories of violence are as varied as the experiences of violence, and the experiences of dealing with violence. Zeinaba Adam, twenty-six, the mother of five children and a resident of one camp in eastern Chad, has suffered from guilt. During a raid on her village in eastern Chad, she asked her husband, Hassein Bourma, to return and retrieve a mattress for her. In his return to the besieged village, he was killed by the Janjaweed—*and she still feels responsible for that. As for her own trauma, Adam said she was shot in five places but believes her headscarf acted as a kind of numinous talisman that protected her. Though she has repeated memories of the incident, trauma counseling has helped her deal with the sense of guilt and responsibility she feels. When I met her, she had just become engaged. She now believes "life is not over. There is life."*

There is unexpected life for Mohammad Abakar, forty-five, a merchant whose eastern Chadian village, D'Jadide, was attacked by the Janjaweed *in August 2006. In the attack, countless women were raped and forty-five villagers were killed. In the ensuing chaos, Abakar refused to give up his horse to a group of men involved in the attack. They hit him repeatedly with an iron pipe and shot him in the face with a Kalashnikov rifle, blinding him in one eye. He was tied up, stabbed, and left to die. Eventually Abakar was found and hospitalized. Like Adam, Abakar attributes a divine hand at work in his survival. "It was God, Allah," he said. Still, Abakar thinks of exacting vengeance for what happened to him. At one point during his recovery, Abakar saw one of the men who shot him at a market, and wanted him dead. The humanitarian worker counseling him said, "This is not the solution. Killing the man will not bring your eye back. If you kill this man, it will be another problem for you."*

Abakar approached the authorities and eventually his assailant was arrested—but later the man was released. Abakar, who says he has "lost everything" in his life, wants full reimbursement from the assailant for his expenses and debts. Only if this demand is fulfilled will Abakar forgive his assailant and say that he and the man "can be brothers." If he does not? Abakar said he will avenge his assault, stab and shoot the man in the face. Does he believe, looking beyond his own experience, that it would be possible for his people and the Arabs to reconcile? With a finger pointed, he answered with a sharp "No." He and others were forcibly displaced and "cannot now move one kilometer from here." Armed men are surrounding them and taking over their land. Even if they could farm in their home villages, he believes those he calls "the Arabs" would now say, "The land doesn't belong to them. It belongs to us." Abakar said there is little they can do except wait "and see what God does in our favor."

✦   ✦   ✦

Finding Solutions Together

The young counselor who has helped Abaker is Neldjagaye Modjingar, sometimes called Oliver. He is twenty-eight, a Christian, from Chad's south who has himself experienced something of the hard side of life, including the political persecution of his family in the 1980s. Like Esther Isaac, Modjingar believes that life experience has given him a sense of empathy. Modjingar is keenly aware of how easily ethnic and religious differences can be exploited and manipulated. Modjingar agrees with Isaac: in the end, those working and those being assisted need "to find solutions together." He also believes that for those recovering from trauma, God has not abandoned them. "God," he said, "is always with them."

This is not an easy realization. One of Modjingar's other clients, Aichata Togolo, a woman in her forties, is still recovering from the murder of her husband, Mahamat Zene, a farmer in the village of Mafakata, Chad, on October 9, 2006. Zene, described by his widow as a "large man," was murdered in front of her—in this case, his throat cutting was followed by a taunt seared in her memory: "We have killed your ugly husband." In an act of quiet ablution, Togolo wrapped her husband's body in a simple cloth and buried him, alone.

Togolo has a distant look in her eyes and rarely looks up from the ground when speaking to a stranger. She has tried to cope by drinking—unusual for a woman in Chad and not the ideal way of dealing with the situation, she acknowledges. Her drinking has caused a mild scandal in the camp. (Rumors of homemade alcohol in the camps are common; strict Islamic injunctions about drinking are taken less seriously in Chad and Darfur than in other predominately Islamic nations and regions, I was told.) Even so, Togolo has been advised by Modjingar to recover at her pace and in her own way. Recovery is not easy. By Togolo's own description, she is "up and down. People take me for crazy. I talk a lot to myself." People spurn her, and Togolo feels she has no future. No man finds her attractive, she said. Togolo feels lonely. If it weren't for Modjingar and others who have listened to her, she is not sure what she would do. "Their visits," she said, "give me hope."

I broached the subject of reconciliation. Togolo said that will not be easy, at least for her. "My mind is not settled," she said. Still, she said eventually she wants to reconcile, forgive and forget. "Revenge will not bring my husband back." Such words offered some sense of encouragement, maybe hope for the future. But such hope was dashed later in the day. Togolo and I had been talking in a community center that housed camp supplies. Behind us stood rolled up bundles of straw, fencing that camp residents could use around their shelters. Esther Isaac told me the fencing had been rejected by the displaced people. Why? "Because it was made by the Arabs."

❖   ❖   ❖

War and displacement change people. They change culture. They change what people expect and want. War and displacement have changed the Darfuris and Chadians who have found themselves uprooted, trying to reclaim and recreate their shattered worlds. The displaced feel nostalgia for what was torn away from them in their rural cosmos—but they could not return to their villages the same people.

On some level, the change is rooted in a process of rural people becoming if not wholly *urban people*, at least *townspeople*, as they settle into displacement camps that start to feel, at the very least, like semipermanent communities. In a sense, those in the camps are becoming urbanized, a process that is altering social roles. Such changes are alternatively mourned or celebrated, be they the loss of power and prestige by elderly sheiks, unruly behavior by young men who no longer feel the need to bow to their elders, or the growing ascendancy of women's groups.

I saw a bit of this phenomena at the Goz-Amir camp in eastern Chad, a four-year-old camp for Darfur refugees. Goz Amir looked and felt as if it were nearly permanent. Certainly, it was a strikingly more settled place than newer, nearby camps for the displaced Chadians. Part of this was simply due to time, as well as levels of aid. The Darfuris had been in their camp longer, and had developed more established rhythms and social relations than their Chadian neighbors. Nevertheless, the Darfuris were not out of harm's way. Just weeks before I met her, Rahkia Ismael Khatir, the Darfur refugee whose experiences began our narrative, had seen her shelter and dozens of others wiped out by a fire that had destroyed many of her and her neighbors' possessions.

A group of young men from Darfur sold cigarettes across the path from Khatir's hut. Several were noticeably better dressed than the Chadians. But none seemed happy with life in the camp. They were keenly aware of what they had lost—what one of the young men, Hamit Hachim Ibrahim, called "our former lives" as farmers. While expressing hope that one day they would be able to return to Darfur, none expressed any optimism that they would do so, at least not while the government of Sudan continued in power. "The problem is al-Bashir," said Youssouf Abdallah Yacoub, another of the young men. "He only likes the Arabs. He doesn't like the blacks." He and his friends said there was little they would do in the coming years except continue receiving humanitarian assistance and selling cigarettes. They did not think of themselves as townspeople. Like many in the camps, they took some solace in raising vegetables in gardens scattered along the periphery of the camp. But this only made the contrast between the life of a farmer and a cigarette vendor all the more glaring. "There is a vast difference between this and our former lives," repeated Ibrahim.

A mixture of shame, unspoken rage, possibly fury, and certainly depression seemed to mark these young men. It was as if they knew they were being changed by events and were powerless to do anything about it. By contrast, women I met in the camps of both Chad and Darfur seemed to be far more accepting of the changes they were experiencing. Not that women like Mariam Adam, whom I met in Darfur in 2007, were having easy lives. Far from it. When I spoke to Adam, a forty-year-old grandmother of one and mother of five, she was living in a camp on the outskirts of Zalingei, in West Darfur. Adam looked a good decade, or even two, older than forty, and she had arrived in the camps only months before. She had been displaced some eight months earlier after government and *Janjaweed* attacks killed her husband and her son-in-law. "It's a difficult life," Adam said as she stood outside the entrance of the small, thatched-roofed mud home where she lives with her children and granddaughter. "We don't have anything." Adam spoke slowly and deliberately with a touch of impatience. Her main concern was tending to the needs of her family, and understandably, she had better things to do than to speak to a Western man interviewing her, notebook in hand. She was trying to resolve a dispute over food rations, while acting as the family's sole breadwinner, selling okra and watermelon in a local market.

However, even with these attendant problems, and despite the ever-present threat of sexual assault while gathering firewood, Adam said she had no plans to leave the camp. Her resoluteness was due not only to finding a small measure of safety in a camp where, rightly or naïvely, camp residents feel the presence of humanitarian personnel offers some type of protection. It is also because, as Adam looked beyond the camp borders, she was not convinced her home village would ever be totally safe again. Moreover, even with all of its attendant tensions and terror, confinements and claustrophobia, Adam's camp offers something her own village never had: free schooling for her children. That is no small matter in a region where education has often been out of reach or unavailable for the rural poor. Indeed, it points to one of the issues that rebel groups in Darfur have cited as a cause of grievance against the Sudanese government: Khartoum's long-standing neglect of Darfur.

Mariam Adam, a quiet woman, was a study of contrasts with the outspoken Fatima Adam (no relation) we met earlier. Yet in her quiet, stubborn way, Mariam Adam was standing on similar ground as Fatima Adam. Perhaps the two Adams and other women represent a new voice in Darfur: a militant and agitated anger that, for now, may have nowhere to go. True, it is hard to see how this deeply felt but politically inchoate force can become a "movement" to influence peace negotiations. The camps are still too isolated from each other. One aid worker I met in Darfur suggested the authorities there feel "this hostility all around them." Knowing such anger is brewing might contribute to some kind of leverage at future peace negotiations, he argued. That seems highly unlikely: the government of Sudan has continued to show very little concern for those it has victimized. Nonetheless, the question of long-term peace and security in both Darfur and Chad will eventually have to grapple with the fact that Mariam Adam, Fatima Adam, and others who come from a region where illiteracy is the norm, will be demanding things they did not have before, particularly for their children. "There's a new need felt," a United Nations worker in Chad told me.

On a flight back to the capital of N'Djamena, this UN worker elaborated on this, saying that humanitarian workers always worry about the long-term sustainability of water, sanitation, and food in places like rural Chad. Often, after emergency and aid groups leave, he said, "it is as if the rug is pulled out from under people." But education, he said, is always something of a "benchmark." Even in dire conditions, people have the resources and local knowledge to find water and food. Not so with education. Wise humanitarians know this issue of sustainability is a central problem, even dilemma, in their work. "It is why camps are so problematic," said Christophe Droeven, the Catholic Relief Services country representative to Chad. Droeven touted the successes in Chad: one of the largest humanitarian operations in the world, operations that were saving lives. "Without humanitarian workers it would be a real disaster," he said. True enough. But truer still, he added, was that lasting success would only come if and when Darfuris crossed the border back to Darfur and Chadians are able to return safely to their border villages in Chad. What kind of future existed in these types of environments? Droeven foresaw years of continued violence, displacement, and more camps.

"I don't see the blue sky, no."

In the end, what will remain? Perhaps precious little: the ligne rouge that has marked Darfur and eastern Chad as one of the most violent, insecure places on earth may continue for years, even decades.

At the least, stories will remain—stories like those of Hamsakine Yayah, who was raped by two men after the Janjaweed attacked her village in March of 2007. Yayah recounted the experience in a firm, determined, objective manner—almost as if the experience had happened to someone else. She looked at me, eye to eye, never blinking. A rape counselor who visits Yayah twice a week to check on her said she is a remarkably strong person. She certainly appears strong, but even the strongest have physical and psychological scars that take years to heal—something Yayah is reminded of every day as she copes with continued back and pelvic pain, more than a year after she was attacked.

"Here, I'll tell you what happened," she said as we sat in her small, cramped hut, speaking through two translators. (Yayah spoke to me in Arabic, translated to French then to English). It all happened on March 18, 2007, in the village of Tiero, seventy-five kilometers from her displacement camp near KouKou, Chad, not far from the Chad-Darfur border. It was morning, nearly eleven o'clock, and Yayah and other women were preparing midday tea, sweetened with sugar. They heard shots and soon the village was overwhelmed with violence: dozens of men arrived in vehicles and on horseback; some were attired in military uniforms, others in civilian clothing.

Tiero was not a small village—it had a population of about ten thousand—but it didn't take long before it was decimated. Yayah saw some of the men cutting fellow villagers' throats. Yayah fled Tiero amid confusion: she became separated from her husband and is not sure what happened to two of her eight children; she assumes they perished. One of the two was a twin; his surviving brother cried as we talked. Yayah and others fled on a road. They congregated at a well, then continued walking. She was in the bush; she carried her youngest child. It was extremely hot, she recalled, motioning with her hands. The sun was glaring.

Suddenly, two men approached her. Yayah says if she ever sees the men again she will "recognize them instantly." They were civilians—she called them "Arab." They beat her first, then forced her onto the ground. As one started to penetrate her, the other held a Kalashnikov rifle to her head. They took turns. Yayah was raped for about forty minutes in all; she said if others had not come down a road, causing her attackers to flee, the assault might have continued even longer. All the while, her children were crying. She said she was in shock afterward for three days. She does not know why this happened beyond what she knows about "la guerre," the war: that those she called Arabs have waged war against black farmers like herself and that rape has been used in Darfur and Chad as an extension of war.

Esther Isaac, who oversees the program to assist women in the camp asked, "Why do men do this? Because they want to say, 'I have the power.' They're using it to say 'We have the power in our hands.' Women are powerless. When someone holds a gun to your head, you accept rape," Isaac said. "They are using rape to dehumanize the women." Isaac believes roughly a third of the women in the camps have been raped. Rape continues because of a culture of impunity—as if "nothing will come of it." Punishment for such crimes is rare in Chad or Darfur—"So men feel, 'let's do it,'" she said.

◆   ◆   ◆

An eventual reunion with Yayah's husband ended in acrimony. When she told him what happened, he instantly asked for a divorce and left her—fleeing to, of all places, Sudan. Yayah is a woman of great understatement: all she can say is that she is "annoyed" with him. Her husband's actions made her fully conscious of the social stigma attached to rape. She doesn't talk about it with others, though she knows other women around her are facing the same dilemma. Yayah acknowledges, "In my heart, I'm ashamed," and that in her culture, "It's best to keep this to yourself."

Her counselor, a young Chadian man from the South, said: "It's a very common experience for women to remain silent." Even so, Yayah seemed comfortable sharing her story with me and said she does not mind that it be told beyond the perimeters of her camp—though she is still wary of having her photo taken. "I'm telling this to you so they won't continue doing this to women." Yayah spoke with great appreciation for the young counselor who visits her and makes her "feel at home. I trust this man." But overall, Yayah is now wary and frightened of men. Marriage holds no interest for her any more.

"I want peace," Yayah said. She wants her children to be fed. Yayah wants to live, as she once did, tilling the land and growing vegetables. She is tired of living in a displacement camp and would like to return home. "I'd go back if I knew I'd be safe." But Yayah realizes that is not likely to happen anytime soon. She paused, just as a few drops of late afternoon rain fell. The precipitation did little to cool or freshen the air of a camp now filling with the smoke and haze from dozens of open-air cooking fires.

I asked Yayah about the possibility of any reconciliation with those she calls Arabs. She turned glum, and wagged her finger. "Very difficult," she said. "No—the Arabs have killed many of our people." She continued: "If I were a man, I'd kill the men who did this," she said. "I'd still like to take a knife or stick to them and stab them."

CHAPTER

6

Hoping Against Hope

*Suffering always means pain, disruption, separation, and incom-
pleteness. It can render us powerless and mute, push us to the
borders of hopelessness and despair. Suffering can maim, wither,
and cripple the heart; or, to quote Howard Thurman, it can be a
"spear of frustration transformed into a shaft of light."*

—M. Shawn Copeland, "Wading Through Many Sorrows"
from *A Troubling in My Soul* (1993)

The word "hope" is overused in humanitarian circles, particularly in the United States.
It is a legacy, no doubt, of our commitment to service and a larger culture of American
optimism. My experiences in Darfur have made me all the more careful in using the
word. When I filed a "something-good-is-happening" story about a Darfur education
project in 2005, my Scandinavian colleague and friend, experienced in the ways of the
Sudanese government, rolled his eyes in mock exasperation and said, "You Americans."
It was a gentle rib from a friend, but it has stuck with me. The ribbing seemed even more
pertinent after returning to Darfur in 2007 and then visiting Chad in 2008. After those
trips, answering the inevitable questions—Is there hope for Darfur? Is there hope for
Chad?—proved to be a moment for hedging. I usually said, "It's tough."

That is what I would still say. As I write this in late 2008, the story of Darfur weaves
in and out of the American media with no real consistency: like an ugly phantom, it is
here one moment, then gone for weeks at a time. When it returns, the news is never
good. In an August report, *The New York Times* reported that just as aid groups were
struggling to feed 3 million Darfuris, the government of Sudan was actively exporting
food elsewhere, part of a new agribusiness initiative. According to the *Times* report,

twice as much sorghum was being exported as was imported as part of emergency aid shipments for Darfur. The *Times* quoted scholar and activist Eric Reeves as saying that the anomaly was "one of the least reported and most scandalous features of the Khartoum regime's domestic policies." It was emblematic, he said, of the Sudanese government's strategy to manipulate "national wealth and power to further enrich itself and its cronies, while the marginalized regions of the country suffer from terrible poverty."

Some might say other governments, facing the need for foreign exchange, have done as the Sudanese government has done, which is true enough. But the policy is part of a depressingly grim pattern. A UN report from 2007 pointed out the utter shamelessness of the government of Sudan in painting military aircraft—including planes used to bombard villages—the color white to make them look like United Nations or African Union aircraft. Given such facts, people like my Scandinavian friend know all too well that to express hope about anything linked to the government of Sudan is a fool's game.

What is not foolish is seeing what has happened in Darfur as part of a larger, tragic arc of history. In his final book, Holocaust survivor Primo Levi said that while the "Nazi madness" and the Holocaust it unleashed were unique, violence "'useful' or 'useless,' is there before our eyes."

> In the Third World it is endemic or episodic. It only awaits its new buffoon (there is no dearth of candidates) to organize it, legalize it, declare it necessary and mandatory, and so contaminate the world. Few countries can be considered immune to a future tide of violence generated by intolerance, lust for power, economic difficulties, religious or political fanaticism, and racialist attritions.

Lust for power—that is one way to see events in Darfur, evoking Henry Adams's observation that "power is poison." If we can hold out hope that the other definition of power—of moral suasion—still has potency, we know from Darfur's example that it is hard work. It is *always* hard work: frustrating, thankless, perhaps even Sisyphean, though never futile. As John Prendergast points out, "For the first time in human history, mass movement against a genocide was organized while it happened." That is a credit to the Darfur activist movement, but it is also a sign of how difficult it remains, even today, to channel moral suasion against entrenched political power. What happened in Darfur happened in plain view—and even then, it did not prompt much in the way of a response, other than the balm of humanitarian aid. As some of the Darfur activists have pointed out, the mistaken lesson of Rwanda was thinking that raising an issue could by itself stop a genocide.

The difficulties of meeting political power with moral force should not surprise us. Writing in the Great Depression of 1930s as the embers of one world war were settling and the flames of another were just beginning to kindle, the American theologian Reinhold

Niebuhr observed in *Moral Man and Immoral Society* that "power must be challenged by power." If Niebuhr were alive today, he probably would neither be surprised by events in Darfur nor by the fact that events occurred in plain sight.

In words that are almost prescient, Niebuhr said this:

> While rapid means of communication have increased the breadth of knowledge about world affairs among citizens of various nations, and the general advance of education has ostensibly promoted the capacity to think rationally and justly upon the inevitable conflicts of interest between nations, there is nevertheless little hope of arriving at a perceptible increase of international morality through the growth of intelligence and the perfection of means of communications.

In other words, just because we *know* more—and know more *quickly*—does not mean that we can stop a Darfur. Moral power has a hard time against the exigencies of brute power or the hesitancy of power restrained. In an appearance at Yale University in the spring of 2008, Eric Reeves said: "The people of Darfur do not matter. . . . They are poor, black, Muslim, and sit on no natural resources of any value. You don't get any lower on the geopolitical pecking order than that."

Not only that, the displaced of Darfur and Chad have been rendered even more powerless than they were before. Think of the dehumanization of women like Hamsakine Yayah, the survivor of rape. To those who raped her and to those who ordered and caused the violence that consumed her village, Yayah was not a human being with full rights. Like the millions uprooted, Yayah was rendered a nonperson—galling given the kind of steely determination commingled with confidence and hopefulness that I saw in this young woman, causing me to say, as I bid her farewell, "You're such a strong person."

I was lucky to have spoken to Yayah. For an hour's time in her small hut, I was able to see beyond the stereotypes created by the confluence of disaster and response — which, in the rush of events, humanitarian workers can fall prey to like anyone else. Smart humanitarians are keenly aware of these kinds of contradictions and try their best to overcome them, however imperfectly. "It's so degrading to see people in these situations, like an eighty-year-old having to live under plastic sheeting," said one UN worker. "I always try to tell people, 'I see you not as IDPs, but as human beings, with full rights.'"

That is the hope of humanitarians: a belief that while such action might not overcome the exigencies of naked political power, it can be the foundation for something better— as in the hope evinced and felt in the presence of Fatima Adam and her women's group. These strong and courageous women have not been afraid to publicly embrace a collective identity about surviving rape and demanding change from camp officials and outsiders like myself.

Of course, the women are also struggling with the issue of reconciliation, and they had varying thoughts about that. Not all, including Hamsakine Yayah, agreed it was possible or desirable, given their experiences. Still, all expressed a desire for *peace*, and that is already a step toward what anthropologist Carolyn Nordstrom has called acts of "creative resistance" to violence. Reflecting on efforts for peace in another African country, Mozambique, Nordstrom has argued that even under "the most extreme circumstances, most people work to recreate a viable society, not demolish it," in part because of a pre-occupation "with defusing the cultures of violence" that produced war in the first place. Nordstrom writes, "It is a violence, they stress, that can last far beyond formal military cease-fires. People constantly reminded themselves and others about the insidious nature of violence to reproduce itself, and to destroy worlds and lives in the process."

I have cited examples of peace work in Darfur; let me add one more. Many of the camps for the displaced are located at the edges of villages whose residents belong to Arab tribes. Knowing the potential for conflict aid can produce, some agencies are careful to say early on that assistance must be shared between the groups. Joseph Akwoc, a relief and rehabilitation coordinator in Nyala for the Sudan Council of Churches, told Paul Jeffrey in 2005 that "it's important that humanitarian assistance not create more conflict."

> We're constantly challenging ourselves, asking whether our activities connect people and encourage peace, or whether we support those structures that divide society. It's important that we are conscious of these factors. When you bring aid from the outside you're never objective. It's vital for us to understand the context we're working in, and whether we're supporting peace at the local level.

> The resources we can bring, whether it's water or education, can be an entrance point for peace building. The first thing we do when we begin work in a village is sit down with the community leaders and say, "This is what we can do and it's not just for some people but for all. We want to make sure that you benefit, all of you, from these resources."

These efforts are balanced by other work, including the introduction of conflict resolution and peace-building elements in schools attended by the displaced. Akwoc continues:

> We get the teachers involved in peace-building, give them some training on how they can create peace among the children, Arab and Darfuri, who share the school. Otherwise the Arab children can intimidate the others, or vice versa. We have to help the children learn to live together, and transform their lives from hatred to friendship. These are small things, small steps, but if you can create harmony among the children it's easier to get it planted among the adults.

If these efforts can pay off, and if survivors like Hamsakine Yayah, Fatima Adam and Mariam Adam can find more than just a measure of dignity in their new circumstances, that would represent one bit of hope. Another would be in the example of General Dallaire, who has every reason to be pessimistic about Darfur, and indeed about humanity in general, given what he had seen in Rwanda. Dallaire—who felt he had been face-to-face with the devil in Rwanda and was doing his best to help stop the evil underway in Darfur—said this: "It's the resiliency of the good that ultimately wins out. If there was an iota of doubt about that, I'd be dead. Ultimately, this momentum of human rights will win out over these frictions."

These "frictions" are only too real. One day in the spring of 2008, I received an email from my Scandinavian colleague lamenting all that was wrong in Darfur and suggesting that the well-placed intentions of humanitarians and human rights workers were up against something that was perhaps insurmountable. "We've lost another one," he wrote. That same evening I got off at my New York City subway station stop and saw a handmade poster inviting the public to a Darfur benefit at a local bar. I had to smile and thought to myself: *drink a beer against al-Bashir.* There was encouragement there—a kind of hope. A group of people who had probably never been to Africa, let alone Sudan, were doing a small thing to help their brothers and sisters in Darfur. And those two brief, small experiences on a single day—a pessimistic message from a friend and a gesture of human solidarity, however small and imperfect, seemed to sum up something about Darfur and its attendant responses—its double-edged meanings.

Darfur may bespeak a certain tragedy and tell us things we do not want to hear: about the nature of naked political power, the limits of humanitarian action and mercy, the complexities of international relations, the continued violence that strikes women in particular. But it also tells us of the stubborn persistence of political activists, the ability of survivors to live to a new day, the welcome durability of the prophetic tradition among a "small remnant" in our established faith traditions.

In short, what has happened *in* Darfur and in response *to* Darfur tells us something at once troubling and affirming—something about ourselves, both for ill and for good, about what it means, today, at the beginning of a new century, to be human.

✦   ✦   ✦

Postscript

Two emails of interest came within a span of a day in late September 2008. One, from my Scandinavian friend and colleague, said this:

"Whatever is going to get Darfur and other parts of Sudan out of their current messy misery has eventually got to come from within. Outsiders may help, nurse, support, etc., but the last four to five years have clearly shown that apart from basic humanitarian service delivery we've had very little consistent and informed engagement to offer."

The email from another humanitarian colleague contained a Los Angeles Times *report that residents of Darfur's largest displacement camp were arming themselves following the August attack by Sudanese troops. It quoted Ali Abdel Khaman Tahir, Kalma Camp's head sheik, as saying: "Our anger is stronger than ever."*

"We are like people living inside a fire."

Afterword:
Photographing in Darfur

Paul Jeffrey

Photographing people displaced by the violence in Darfur is not easy. Even getting a visa for Sudan, the first step in getting there, can be a challenge. For my first visit to Darfur in 2005, I chased a visa through several European capitals before a Scandinavian church leader persuaded a Sudanese ambassador to grant me one. And then once inside Sudan, it's illegal for foreigners to take photographs without a special permit from the government; again, more bureaucracy, more waiting, and when the permit comes, it proscribes photographing both the expected—soldiers, bridges, military bases—as well as the impossible to avoid—poor people—almost everyone. Next, one must obtain a government permit to travel to Darfur, in the far west of the country. Many journalists wait for that permit for weeks, and in many cases it never comes unless you are traveling under the auspices of a humanitarian organization operating in the area.

Once you finally get to Darfur, each visit to a camp for internally displaced persons (IDPs) usually requires a government permit requested at least two days in advance. Add in the inevitable logistical difficulties—helicopter flights that get cancelled, four-wheel drive vehicles that get stuck in flooded wadis, trips nixed because of combat in the area, zealous local security officials who detain you for not having the correct permits even though you do, harsh midday light that creates inscrutable shadows on dark faces—and it's surprising you capture any usable images.

Fortunately, the poor want their story told. Those who have survived brutal attacks and been herded into miserable camps want the world to know what they have lived through and how they're living now. So wandering through the camps, where one family's space often yields quickly to the intimate but unmarked confines of another's, I am repeatedly amazed by the hospitality of the poor. That's true in Darfur and in so many violence-ridden corners of our planet. Those who have literally nothing are quick to offer what little they have, a cup of tea or a meager patch of shade, to a pale and sweaty stranger. Such dignity is a strong dissuasion to think of these people as mere victims. Perhaps despair is a privilege of class; busy struggling to survive, the displaced have little time to mourn the life and community they lost to the paroxysm of violence that swept through their lives. Or perhaps they have been so strengthened by their experience of horror that they have moved past being victimized; don't mourn, organize. Or perhaps their dignity flows from the simple fact that these are strong people. The residents of Darfur live in what is in the best of times a harsh environment, yet they have survived and flourished and most of the time gotten along fine with each other for hundreds of years. Whatever the causes, they seem to have little of victim about them.

That dovetails well with an important element of the international code of conduct for humanitarian organizations working in disaster relief. Principle number ten is: "In our information, publicity, and advertising activities, we shall recognize disaster victims as dignified human beings, not hopeless objects." Although selling misery has long been a way for relief groups to raise money, peddling images of people who appear helpless is both unethical and inaccurate. Most human beings bear an enormous reserve of dignity, even when raped, robbed, and chased from their homes and herded into camps where they have to depend on the compassion of others to survive. I hope the images in this book reflect in some way the strength of the women, men, and children who are the survivors of the Darfur genocide.

Others have photographed in Darfur. James Nachtwey's compelling images from Darfur in 2004 were among the first to show the world a people living through the hell of displacement. Brian Steidle, although not a photographer, leveraged his unique access as a military advisor into making available photos of burning villages and ravaged corpses, including unforgettable images of young girls handcuffed and burned to death outside their school. That the world didn't do enough in response to what it saw in those photos is an indictment of how jaded and complicit with violence we have become. Other journalists have crossed the dodgy border from Chad to capture images of ragtag rebel bands, often risking their lives to get the story out. Still others have come into the region embedded with the African Union mission.

My access to the people of Darfur, and to the refugees in eastern Chad, took place because of my work with an alliance of church-based agencies responding to emergencies around the world. I entered Darfur with relief workers trying at the most basic level to keep the displaced and refugees alive, and beyond that to equip them with education and skills that will encourage a better quality life in the long-term. This faith-based alliance has also fostered a rather unique labor of trying to recover some of the atrophied conflict-resolution mechanisms that existed throughout the region before the current government in Khartoum centralized authority and thus disabled local initiatives at reconciliation. This peace-building work afforded me access to some Arab communities that otherwise are often ignored by relief organizations.

So you won't find here photos of *Janjaweed* militias on horseback, nor of rebel commanders, their faces swaddled against the desert sun by camouflaged scarves. What you will find are images of everyday life for the 2.5 million people who survived the genocidal attacks on their villages and who now wait in sweltering camps for the day when they can return home to rebuild their lives in peace. They have not given up, despite all the odds against them. They continue to get up every morning and offer their prayers of thanks for a new day before beginning their ritual of chores and study and play that will get them through until the night comes again. Their quiet determination to survive is a sturdy counterpoint to the torrent of words over Darfur that is generated daily in the far corners of our world. Their refusal to die, no matter that it's the fate that Khartoum clearly intends for them, is a powerful sign that our solidarity needs new urgency. Their thirst for life encourages us to take a moment to be thankful for our homes and communities, and then, that moment ended, calls us to a new level of effective solidarity that makes real the cry of "never again."

Bibliography

Abramowitz, Michael. "U.S. Promises on Darfur Don't Match Actions: Bush Expresses Passion for Issue, but Policies Have Been Inconsistent." *The Washington Post*, October 29, 2007.

Andersson, Hilary. "China 'is fuelling war in Darfur.'" BBC, July 13, 2008. http://news.bbc.co.uk/2/hi/africa/7503428.stm

Anderson, Scott. "How Did Darfur Happen?" *The New York Times Magazine*, October 17, 2004.

Borger, Julian. "Scorched." *Guardian*, April 28, 2007. http://www.guardian.co.uk/environment/2007/apr/28/sudan.climatechange

Bock, Christian W.D., and Miller, Leland R. "Darfur: Where Is Europe?" *The Washington Post*, December 9, 2004. http://www.washingtonpost.com/wp-dyn/articles/A49825-2004Dec8.html

Dallaire, Roméo. *Shake Hands with the Devil: The Failure of Humanity in Rwanda.* New York: Carroll & Graf Publishers, 2004.

de Waal, Alex. "A Cross-Border Marketplace of Loyalties" from "Making Sense of Darfur," Social Science Research Council, June 21, 2008. http://www.ssrc.org/blogs/darfur/2008/06/21/a-cross-border-marketplace-of-loyalties/

———. "The Humanitarian Carnival: A Celebrity Vogue." *World Affairs Journal*, Fall 2008. At: http://www.worldaffairsjournal.org/2008%20-%20Fall/comments/comments-DeWaal.html

———. *War in Darfur and the Search for Peace.* Cambridge: Global Equity Initiative, Harvard University, 1992.

———. "Counter-insurgency on the Cheap." *London Review of Books*, August 5, 2004.

———. "Origins of the Darfur Crisis of 2003–4." *ACAS Bulletin* 72 (Winter 2005–Spring 2006): http://acas.prairienet.org/bulletin/bull72-02-deWaal.html

Deng, Francis. *War of Visions: Conflict of Identities in Sudan.* Washington, D.C.: Brookings Institution, 1995.

"Dueling Over Darfur" (Online debate between Alex de Waal and John Prendergast). *Newsweek*, November 8, 2007. http://www.newsweek.com/id/69004

Farley, Maggie. "Envoy Sees Little Darfur Hope Now." *Los Angeles Times*, June 25, 2008.

Gettleman, Jeffrey. "The Food Chain: Darfur Withers as Sudan Sells Food." *The New York Times,* August 10, 2008. http://www.nytimes.com/2008/08/10/world/africa/10sudan.html?scp=1&sq=The%20Food%20Chain%20%20darfur&st=cse

Gettleman, Jeffrey, and Lydia Polgreen. "Sudan Rallies Behind Leader Reviled Abroad." *The New York Times*, July 28, 2008. http://www.nytimes.com/2008/07/28/world/africa/28sudan.html

Hamilton, Rebecca, and Hazlett, Chad. "'Not on Our Watch': The Emergence of the American Movement for Darfur," in Alex de Waal, ed., *War in Darfur and the Search for Peace*. Cambridge, MA: Global Equity Initiative, Harvard University, 1992.

Herlinger, Chris. "Stuck in Darfur: Refugees Are 'Like Hens in Cages.'" *The Christian Century*, February 8, 2005.

———. "Darfur: Fear and Chaos in a Fragile Land." *National Catholic Reporter*, April 1, 2005.

———. "Darfur's Unfinished Story." *Harvard Divinity Bulletin* (Autumn 2005): 76–86.

———. "Darfur: Return to an Unsettled Land." *National Catholic Reporter*, September 28, 2007.

———. "A New Voice in Darfur." *Harvard Divinity Bulletin* (Winter 2008):

Heschel, Abraham Joshua. "The Reasons for My Involvement in the Peace Movement." from *Moral Grandeur and Spiritual Audacity*. Essays edited by Susannah Heschel. New York: Farrar, Straus and Giroux, 1996.

Jeffrey, Paul. "Rape: A Tool of War in Sudan." *Response*, October 2005, pp. 20-25.

———. "Waiting in Darfur." *The Christian Century*, October 2, 2007.

Kristof, Nicholas. "The Pope and Hypocrisy." *The New York Times*, April 6, 2005. http://www.nytimes.com/2005/04/06/opinion/06kristof.html

Levi, Primo. *The Drowned and the Saved*. New York: Vintage International, 1989.

Nawyn, William E. *American Protestantism's Response to Germany's Jews and Refugees, 1933–1941*. Ann Arbor, MI: UMI Research Press, 1981.

Niebuhr, Reinhold. *Moral Man and Immoral Society*. New York: Charles Scribner's Sons, 1932.

Nordstrom, Carolyn. "The Dirty War: Civilian Experience of Conflict in Mozambique and Sri Lanka." In Kumar Rupasinghe, ed., *Internal Conflict and Governance*, pp. 27–43. New York: St. Martin's Press, 1992.

———. *A Different Kind of War Story: An Ethnography of Political Violence*. Philadelphia: University of Pennsylvania Press, 1997.

Power, Samantha. *A Problem from Hell: America and the Age of Genocide*. New York: Basic Books, 2002.

———. "Remember Rwanda but Take Action in Sudan." *The New York Times*. April 6, 2004. http://query.nytimes.com/gst/fullpage.html?res=990DEFD61E39F935 A35757C0A9629C8B63

Prunier, Gérard. *Darfur: The Ambiguous Genocide*. Ithaca, NY: Cornell University Press. 2005.

Rieff, David. "Humanitarian Vanities." *The New York Times Magazine*, June 1, 2008.

———. "Humanitarian Intervention." Crimes of War Project. http://www. crimesofwar.org/thebook/humanitarian-intervention.html

Silverstein, Ken. "Sudanese Visitor Split U.S. Officials." *Los Angeles Times*, June 17, 2005. http://articles.latimes.com/2005/jun/17/world/fg-sudan17

Tubiana, Jérôme. "The Chad-Sudan Proxy War and the 'Darfurization' of Chad: Myths and Reality." Geneva: Small Arms Survey, April 2008. http://www.smallarms-survey.org/files/portal/spotlight/sudan/Sudan_pdf/SWP%2012%20Chad%20Sudan%20Proxy%20War.pdf

United Nations. Copy of Resolution 1674 (2006). Adopted by the Security Council on April 28, 2006. http://domino.un.org/UNISPAl.NSF/361eea1cc08301c485256cf600606959/e529762befa456f8852571610045ebef!OpenDocument

———. Report of the International Commission of Inquiry on Darfur to the United Nations Secretary-General. Geneva: January 25, 2005, http://www.un.org/News/dh/sudan/com_inq_darfur.pdf .

Wax, Emily. "Sudan's Ragtag Rebels." *The Washington Post*, September 7, 2004.